You're Re
the Wrong L

D0546997

DISCARDED

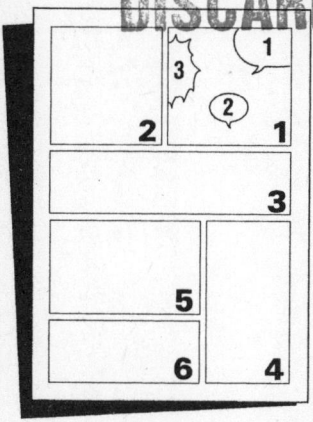

Whoops! Guess what? You're starting at the wrong end of the comic!

...It's true! In keeping with the original Japanese format, **Blue Exorcist** is meant to be read from right to left, starting in the upper-right corner.

Unlike English, which is read from left to right, Japanese is read from right to left, meaning that action, sound effects and word-balloon order are completely reversed... something which can make readers unfamiliar with Japanese feel pretty backwards themselves. For this reason, manga or Japanese comics published in the U.S. in English have sometimes been published "flopped"—that is, printed in exact reverse order, as though seen from the other side of a mirror.

By flopping pages, U.S. publishers can avoid confusing readers, but the compromise is not without its downside. For one thing, a character in a flopped manga series who once wore in the original Japanese version a T-shirt emblazoned with "M A Y" (as in "the merry month of") now wears one which reads "Y A M"! Additionally, many manga creators in Japan are themselves unhappy with the process, as some feel the mirror-imaging of their art skews their original intentions.

We are proud to bring you Kazue Kato's **Blue Exorcist** in the original unflopped format. For now, though, turn to the other side of the book and let the adventure begin...!

—Editor

In the next volume...

The tragic story of what happened to Rin and Yukio's mother, Yuri Egin, continues to unfold. Yuri and Father Fujimoto were once up-and-coming young Exorcists involved in Section 13's extensive operation to research elixirs of immortality and develop clones to house the spirits of demons. The project seemed to be moving ahead until the unexpected manifestation of a demonic spirit into one of the clone bodies. And this wasn't just any demon—the entity seemed to be the most powerful demon of all: Satan!

Coming February 2020!

BLUE EXORCIST

BLUE EXORCIST VOL. 22
SHONEN JUMP Manga Edition

STORY & ART BY KAZUE KATO

Translation & English Adaptation/John Werry
Touch-up Art & Lettering/John Hunt, Primary Graphix
Cover & Interior Design/Julian [JR] Robinson
Editor/Mike Montesa

AO NO EXORCIST © 2009 by Kazue Kato
All rights reserved.
First published in Japan in 2009 by SHUEISHA Inc., Tokyo.
English translation rights arranged by SHUEISHA Inc.

The stories, characters and incidents mentioned in this publication are entirely fictional.

No portion of this book may be reproduced or transmitted in any form or by any means without written permission from the copyright holders.

Printed in the U.S.A.

Published by VIZ Media, LLC
P.O. Box 77010
San Francisco, CA 94107

10 9 8 7 6 5 4 3 2 1
First printing, September 2019

PARENTAL ADVISORY
BLUE EXORCIST is rated T+ for Older Teen and is recommended for ages 16 and up. It contains violence, suggestive situations and some adult themes.

Kazue Kato

This volume begins to explore Shiro's and Yuri's pasts as they relate to the Blue Night. Even if I push the story along at a fast pace, it looks like it could get long. But I have to pay sufficient attention to certain events, so I'm going to pace myself like I'm in a race.

Enjoy the manga!

Dark History

4-panel comics are back!

It don't matter to me.
Okay, okay!
That's right! And the lack of time is making me skimp in places like this!

Art Staff

Erika Uemura

Ryoji Hayashi

Mari Oda

Sai Yamagishi

Aki Shiina

Art Assistants

Yamanaka-san

Obata-san

Yoshiyama-kun

Sasaki-kun

Editors

Tadahiro Fukushima

Shihei Lin (in charge of media)

Graphic Novel Editor

Ryusuke Kuroki

Graphic Novel Design

Shimada Hideaki

Daiju Asami (L.S.D.)

Manga

Kazue Kato

(In no particular order)
(Note: The caricatures and statements are from memory!)

When volume 23 comes out next year, *Blue Exorcist* will be celebrating its tenth anniversary!! And it's all thanks to you, readers!!

THANK YOU FOR THIS QUESTION! FOR THE MOST PART, I DON'T MODEL THE CHARACTERS, WHETHER BOYS OR GIRLS, ON REAL PEOPLE.

I LOVE THE WAY THE MALE CHARACTERS HAVE INCREDIBLY REALISTIC PERSONALITIES. DID YOU BASE THEM ON YOUR OWN SIBLINGS OR OTHER REAL BOYS?

DANDELION (?), TOKYO PREFECTURE

NEXT QUESTION !!

GYAAAAAH !!

HEY, YOU !!

LORD LUCIFERRRRR !!

GASP... KOFF CHOKE GAG KOFF KOFFFF !!

YEP.

IT'S A TOUPEE.

GEDOIN ISN'T IN THE MAIN MANGA ANYMORE, BUT I REGULARLY HEAR FROM PEOPLE WHO WONDER ABOUT HIM—WHICH MAKES ME HAPPY! BUT HAVING HIM SHOW UP HERE WOULD BE A HASSLE, SO I'LL HAVE THE THREE OTHERS WHO WERE THERE PROVIDE ACCOUNTS.

WELL, THAT'S ALL FOR NOW!!

YIIIKES !!!

OKAY! GRAH!

HORNS ??! BUT THEY LOOK LIKE GOOSE EGGS! IF YOU WERE GONNA GIVE ME HORNS, YOU SHOULD'VE MADE THEM LOOK COOLER!

HORNS.

I SUPPOSE FULLY AWAKENING AS SATAN'S NEPHILIM IS HAVING AN EFFECT ON YOUR BODY. I SUSPECT IT'S LIKE HOW YOUR HAIR COLOR CHANGED, BUT WHAT ARE THEY REALLY?

HM? (PAT PAT) WHOA! YOU'RE RIGHT! THEY'RE HARD! IS THAT BONE? ARE THEY GOOSE EGGS? SCARY!

WHAT ARE THOSE THINGS LIKE HORNS ON RIN'S FOREHEAD?

TM OF TIME (12), FUKUOKA PREFECTURE

BUT I DO WANT TO CREATE CHARACTERS THAT RESONATE WITH READERS AND MAKE THEM SAY, "I TOTALLY UNDERSTAND!" OR "I KNOW PEOPLE LIKE THAT!" SO I'M HAPPY IF THEY COME ACROSS AS EVEN A LITTLE REALISTIC. AND I DO HAVE A BROTHER!

I SEEM TO REMEMBER THAT I STARTED TO CALL YOU "BIG BROTHER" WHEN I WAS LITTLE BECAUSE I HEARD FATHER FUJIMOTO AND THE PEOPLE AT THE MONASTERY SAY THINGS LIKE, "RIN, YOU'RE HIS BIG BROTHER, RIGHT?" AND "YOU'RE HIS BIG BROTHER, SO DO YOUR BEST," WHEN THEY CHIDED OR COMFORTED YOU.

HUH? REALLY ?!

OH WELL. I'VE HEARD THAT THE TWINS OFTEN CALL EACH OTHER BY THEIR FIRST NAMES. IN THE ENGLISH TRANSLATION, I ACTUALLY USUALLY CALL YOU "RIN."

THESE ARE THE BONUS PAGES. AS A RULE, WE DON'T BRING IN STUFF FROM THE ACTUAL MANGA.

I DO OFTEN SPEAK TO YOU.

HMM, I WONDER ...

COME ON... ANOTHER ONE?!

WHEN DID YUKIO START CALLING RIN HIS "BIG BROTHER"?

INDIGO EXORCIST (26), IWATE PREFECTURE

WHAAAAAH ?!

ON PAGES 62 AND 63 OF VOLUME 15, THERE'S A SCENE WHERE LUCIFER MAKES MICHAEL GEDOIN DISAPPEAR. WHY DID ONLY HIS HAIR REMAIN? SURELY IT WASN'T A WIG! OR WOULD HAIR JUST FALL IN ONE PIECE LIKE THAT? AND NOT FALL APART?

I LOVE EXERCISE ♡ (12), NAGASAKI PREFECTURE

I'M NOT EMBARRASSED !!

C'MON, DON'T BE EMBARRASSED.

WHY?! I DON'T WANT TO!

TCH! OKAY... AS A TEST, CALL ME RIN!

WELL, THESE ARE THE BONUS PAGES. AS A RULE, WE DON'T BRING IN STUFF FROM THE ACTUAL MANGA.

HEY, ISN'T IT ABOUT TIME WE STOPPED FIGHTING AND GOT ALONG? FIGHTING IS A PAIN.

YEAH ...

OH...COME TO THINK OF IT, WHEN I WAS LITTLE, THEY DID SAY STUFF LIKE THAT TO ME A LOT. IF THEY SAID, "TRY HARDER, BECAUSE YOU'RE YUKIO'S BIG BROTHER," THEN I WOULD TRY HARDER, SO THEY SAID IT TO ME ALL THE TIME. THAT SURE BRINGS BACK MEMORIES!

IN VOLUME 16, IT SEEMS LIKE THE THREE WISE MONKEYS ARE SERVING MEPHISTO. DOES THAT MEAN THEY'RE KIN OF THE KING OF TIME? OR IF YOU BECOME ONE OF THE BAAL, CAN YOU MAKE DEMONS WITH OTHER ATTRIBUTES OBEY YOU?

MOITOI (17), SHIGA PREFECTURE

ACTUALLY, THOUGH, I DIDN'T REALLY GET MUCH OF THAT!

WELL, AT LEAST YOU'RE MATTER-OF-FACT ABOUT IT.

SO, UM... ANYWAY, YOU DON'T KNOW WHICH I'LL BE, RIGHT? I HOPE I DIE NATURALLY.

MOST FIRST-GENERATION NEPHILIM LIVE A LONG TIME. DEPENDING ON THEIR CHARACTERISTICS, HOWEVER, THERE ARE CASES OF THEIR BODIES NOT LASTING. THEN THEY DIE, SORT OF LIKE HOW BODIES POSSESSED BY DEMONS RAPIDLY WEAKEN.

THAT COULD HAPPEN ?!

WELL, I DON'T THINK "FOREVER" IS POSSIBLE. I'VE HEARD THAT EVEN A LONG-LIVED NEPHILIM CAN ONLY LIVE ABOUT 200 YEARS. WHETHER A DEMON OR SOME OTHER LIFE-FORM, ALL MATTER CRUMBLES TO DUST. HOWEVER, YOU'RE THE FIRST NEPHILIM OF SATAN, SO I HAVE NO IDEA WHAT WILL HAPPEN. YOU MIGHT LIVE ON FOR ETERNITY OR YOUR BODY MIGHT GIVE OUT SOON.

SORRY. TO BE HONEST, I HAVEN'T COUNTED. BUT I DOUBT IT'S UNDER 50.

I UNDERSTAND YOUR CHAGRIN. I WAS GOING THROUGH A LOT AROUND THAT TIME TOO. BUT THE QUESTION CORNER HAS DEALT YOU THIS QUESTION, SO DON'T BE EMBARRASSED AND JUST TELL US.

HUH?! A QUESTION FOR ME?! IN SEARCH OF POWER, I TURNED MY BACK ON TRUE CROSS ACADEMY AND MY OLDER BROTHER AND WENT TO THE ILLUMINATI. BUT YOU WANT TO KNOW HOW MANY LOVE LETTERS I GET? WHAT'S THE BIG IDEA?!

HOW MANY TIMES HAS YUKIO RECEIVED A LOVE LETTER?

THE GREEN KNIGHT (12), OSAKA PREFECTURE

FOR THE MOST PART, WE KINGS CAN ONLY USE OUR OWN KIN AS SUBORDINATES. BUT WE CAN USE DEMONS WITH OTHER ATTRIBUTES IF WE ASK THE KING OF THAT ELEMENT. SO IT'S IMPOSSIBLE FOR A KING TO BORROW DEMONS FROM A KING HE DOESN'T GET ALONG WELL WITH, BUT A KING CAN OFTEN BORROW FROM KINGS HE DOES GET ALONG WITH. IN MY CASE, I CAN BORROW DEMONS OF EARTH, INSECTS AND SPIRIT, BUT I CAN'T BORROW FROM LIGHT, FIRE, WATER AND ROT. THE THREE WISE MONKEYS DON'T BELONG TO ANY ELEMENT, SO I CAN REQUEST THEIR AID WHENEVER I WANT. I ACTUALLY GET ALONG WITH LOTS OF UNAFFILIATED DEMONS. THERE AREN'T MANY TIME DEMONS, SO THEY AREN'T VERY CONVENIENT.

BUT THAT'S AN *ABNORMAL* AMOUNT.

OH...BUT AFTER I'VE EXERCISED A LOT, I'M SUPER HUNGRY, SO I EAT A TON OF MEAT AND RICE. I CAN GOBBLE UP FIVE SERVINGS IN NO TIME!

YES, THAT'S A NORMAL AMOUNT FOR A HIGH SCHOOL BOY.

HOW MUCH? ME? UM...A NORMAL AMOUNT? I HAVE BREAKFAST AND EAT ABOUT THREE BREAD THINGIES BEFORE LUNCH. AFTER SCHOOL, I STOP BY THE DORM TO MAKE ABOUT FIVE RICE BALLS FOR TAKING TO CRAM SCHOOL. CLASSES FINISH ABOUT EIGHT OR NINE AT NIGHT, AND MY STOMACH IS KILLING ME BY THEN. SO WHEN I GET HOME, I EAT A LATE SUPPER. THAT'S NORMAL, RIGHT?

HOW MUCH DOES RIN EAT?

YUMI-RIINA (18), NIIGATA PREFECTURE

ALL RIGHT, LET'S KICK OFF VOLUME 22'S *QUESTORCIST!*

BLUE QUESTORCIST

YEAH. I DOUBT LIVING FOREVER WOULD BE A VERY HAPPY LIFE.

HUH? AM I REALLY GONNA LIVE THAT LONG?! I DON'T WANNA LIVE ON AFTER EVERYONE ELSE DIES! THAT'D SUCK!

AFTER ALL, WE'RE TALKIN' ABOUT SATAN! SO I BET YOU WILL! I'D BE INTERESTED TO KNOW, BUT I DOUBT I'LL LIVE LONG ENOUGH TO FIND OUT. TOO BAD.

HUH? SERIOUSLY ?!

RIN OKUMURA IS A FIRST-GENERATION NEPHILIM BORN OF SATAN AND A HUMAN BEING, SO I BET HE'LL LIVE A LONG TIME.

PEOPLE WHO ARE HALF DEMON AND HALF HUMAN ARE CALLED NEPHILIM, AND THE FIRST GENERATION INHERITS THE MOST POWER. BUT IF THE SECOND AND THIRD GENERATIONS' PARTNERS ARE HUMAN, THEIR CHILDREN'S DEMONIC ABILITIES WILL BE WEAKER.

I HEAR THEY DO. MY FAMILY HAS FOX-GOD BLOOD, AND I'VE HEARD THE FIRST GENERATION LIVED A LONG TIME. BUT MY GRANDMOTHER WAS THE 63RD GENERATION, AND SHE PASSED AWAY AT AGE 77, SO I DOUBT I'LL LIVE VERY LONG.

DEMONS LIVE A LONG TIME, SO DO HUMANS WHO HAVE INHERITED DEMON BLOOD ALSO LIVE A LONG TIME?

FULL-POWER SO-SO (14), FUKUOKA PREFECTURE

BONUS

Ugh... I'm sleepy!
I get sleepy in the past too?!
You also have a sleeping bag
How thoughtful of you!

BLUB
BLUB
BLUB
BLUE EXORCIST 22 - END -

GYAIIEE! THIS IS TOO EMBARRASSING! I CAN'T WATCH!!
GAAA!
IS THIS GONNA WORK OUT?!
What the ...?!
GOOD QUESTION.
FWAAAP
I CAN'T BELIEVE THIS!
WHAT'S GOING TO HAPPEN BETWEEN THEM?!
"BUT DON'T FORGET. THIS JOURNEY LEADS TO TRAGEDY."
HOWEVER WILL IT END?
NEXT.
GLUB GLUB
GLUB GLUB
ADMINISTRATION OF GENERAL ANESTHESIA IS COMPLETE.
THEN BEGIN THE PENETRATION EXPERIMENT WITH ELIXIR 97 ON GORO...
...SUBJECT AO-005.

AIN'T HAPPENIN'.
GASP
Long time no see!
TEE HEE!
...PROTECTING ME?
ARE YOU...
HE...
...REJECTED ME.

I'M IN LOVE WITH YOU, SHIRO.
Heh! YOU'RE JUST A KID...
I'M 16.
BLUSH
HOW OLD ARE YOU?!
Y... YOU...

I...

HORRIBLE?
YOU DIDN'T HAVE ANY PARENTS.
DON'T BE DUMB! IT'S NORMAL!
AND IT DOESN'T MATTER!
YOUR BROTHERS AND SISTERS SUFFERED...
...AND YOU WERE FRIGHTENED.
YEAH, IT SUCKS...
...BUT IT'S NO BIG DEAL!

SO I CAN'T STAND IT WHEN SOMEONE CALLS ME WEAK!!
DON'T EVER SAY THAT AGAIN!
WHAT'S THAT LOOK ON YOUR FACE?
YOU'VE HAD A HORRIBLE TIME.
?!

THE FIRST THING I REMEMBER...
WAH
NYOOO
BUT A CAREFREE DIMWIT LIKE YOU WOULDN'T UNDERSTAND.
...I WAS DRUGGED AND IN CONFINEMENT.
WE DIDN'T HAVE PARENTS TO PROTECT US.
ONE BY ONE, MY BROTHERS AND SISTERS WENT CRAZY AND DIED.
I ONLY SURVIVED BECAUSE I WAS STRONG.

THAT'S RIGHT!! EVERY DAY IS A BLAST!
YEAH!!
...
KAW
KAW
AT LEAST THERE'S A DEPARTMENT FOR FREAKS LIKE YOU WHO LOVE DEMONS, YEAH?
I LOVE GOLEMS
LOOK AT THIS GOLEM I MADE!
ISN'T IT CUTE?
FAMILIARS AREN'T PETS.
NEE
NEE
IF YOU SHOW THE SLIGHTEST WEAKNESS, THEY'LL ATTACK.
THE WEAK CAN'T SURVIVE.
Nee! Nee!
PEOPLE USE WEAKLINGS AS TOOLS AND THEN KILL THEM.

KAW
KAW
KAW
GUAAH
OHHH...
...THIS IS A DEMON FARM, EH?
...
Moo!! Moo! Nee! Nee!
Moo!! Nee!
IT'S MY FIRST TIME HERE AND I ALREADY HATE IT.
DON'T SWEAT IT.
TAP
??
WHAT DO YOU WANT?
You're such a delinquent
SORRY ABOUT THE OTHER DAY.
I BARELY KNOW YOU, BUT I YELLED AT YOU AND SLAPPED YOU.

RINKA...
HUH?
WILL-O'-THE-WISP?!
ARE YOU ALL RIGHT, FUJIMOTO?
CHATTER
!!
OW!
?!
WHAT WAS THAT?!
HWUP
HEY! OSCEOLA! PUT ME DOWN!!
?!
ARGH!
HWUP
RIGHT!
THROW THEM IN THE TRUCK! THIS MERITS PUNISHMENT!
IT DOESN'T MATTER!
KAW KAW
KAW
KAW
KAW

YOU TREAT THE WHOLE WORLD LIKE YOUR ENEMY!
IF YOU KEEP ACTING LIKE THIS, YOU REALLY WILL END UP ALONE!
KNOCK IT OFF!!
FUJIMOTO!
AH!

WELL, ONLY WEAKLINGS TAKE IT OUT ON OTHERS!!
GRAB
YOU'RE THE BRAT!
YOU LITTLE BRAT!!!
TRY SAYING THAT AGAIN!
YURI!!
STOP IT!
HEY...

SMAK
YOU WEAKLING !!!!
YOU THINK YOU'VE SUFFERED A LOT?!
HUH ?!

G-GOOD WORK, FUJIMOTO!!
WSH
DESTROYING IT WAS THE BEST OPTION!
THOK
GRNF!
IT'S COLD, SO-
HERE, HAVE THIS!
RICK!!
Who're you?!
DON'T TALK TO ME...
FUJI-MOTO!
FWUMP
...YOU LOW-RANKING SCUM!
TNK

YOU DID WELL, YURI EGIN.
AND YOU'RE AMBITIOUS.
AMBITIOUS?
I CAN'T BELIEVE YOU'RE ONLY JUNIOR SECOND CLASS.
SHALL I TALK TO THE HIGHER-UPS?
UM!
SORRY, BUT I LIKE DEMONS, SO I DON'T WANT TO FIGHT THEM.
HA HA!
OH...
...YOU'RE ONE OF THOSE ECCENTRICS, HUH?
IT'S DISGUSTING!
YOU'RE UNRELIABLE! AND A HYPOCRITE!
SO DON'T GET COCKY!
FUJIMOTO, I'VE MADE MY DECISION. ARE YOU DISPLEASED?
SHE JUST GOT LUCKY, THAT'S ALL!!

אמת
!
AN AMATEURISH AND INCOMPLETE SEAL...
WOW...
RIP
RIP
SOMEONE TURNED YOU INTO A GOLEM.
REST NOW.
RRIP
KTUNK

GRAA
GRAA
GRAA
VWP
VWP
VWP
AAH
AAH
VWP
VWP

THOOM
THOOM
THOOM
THOOM
WATCH OUT!!
GR
AAH
G
A
A

RMM
RMM
CAN WE LEAVE THIS TO A SMALL, UNARMED GIRL?
DON'T LOOK DOWN ON WOMEN! IF ANYTHING HAPPENS, WE'LL JUMP IN.
PEH!
I BET SHE'LL RUN FOR HER LIFE!
RMM

WHO ARE YOU?
YURI EGIN, JUNIOR EXORCIST SECOND CLASS.
I'M HERE AS A TRAINER OF FAMILIARS.
...
!
WELL, YOU GOT ANY IDEAS?
TH-THAT GIANT STATUE...
COULD IT BE A GOLEM?
WE CONSIDERED THAT BUT REJECTED IT.
It's 500 years old!
A GOLEM NEEDS A MASTER, BUT ITS MASTER WOULD BE DEAD BY NOW.
I UNDERSTAND THAT...
...BUT MAYBE SOMEONE ALIVE TODAY IS CONTROLLING IT.
WHEN GOLEMS DON'T FEEL THREATENED, THEY CALM DOWN.
SO PLEASE! LET ME CHECK!

GRA A
THOOM
THOOM
THERE'S A VILLAGE JUST 300 METERS AWAY!
DON'T THEY UNDERSTAND ?!
IT'S AN IMPORTANT ARCHEOLOGICAL RELIC.
THE MEXICAN GOVERNMENT HAS REQUESTED THAT WE EXORCIZE IT WITHOUT DESTROYING IT.
AA
THRUM THRUM
RATTLE RATTLE
THOOM
WE CAN'T EXORCIZE AN UNKNOWN EVIL GHOST!
WE DON'T EVEN KNOW WHAT KIND OF DEMON IT IS.
UGH... WHAT A PAIN...
IT COULD BE A GALATEA OR FETISH.
NO. THERE HAVEN'T BEEN ANY FIRE ATTACKS.
COULD IT BE COATLICUE, THE AZTEC EARTH GODDESS?
THOOM
OUT OF THE QUESTION! IT WOULD TARNISH THE ORDER'S IMAGE!
THE ARCHAEOLOGISTS CAN PICK UP THE PIECES!
UM...
IT'D BE FASTER TO JUST DESTROY IT.
FUJIMOTO...
I'LL GO BLOW IT TO BITS.

DADA
DUM
DUM
THIS IS A MISSION THAT TOOK PLACE 29 YEARS AGO IN MEXICO.
DUM
DUM DADA
DUM DADA
DUM DADA
THOOM
GR
A
A
WSH
RUN!!
THOOM
THOOM
IT'S NO USE!
KTOOM
TCH! A PACIFICATION CEREMONY DIDN'T WORK EITHER!

I THINK HE LOOKS LONELY.
REALLY?
And he's my age...
UNLIKE US, HE'S COOL!
HE'S SENIOR FIRST CLASS! AND HE'S THE EXORCISM SUBSECTION MANAGER!
SLAW
SO BORING!
GIMME A BREAK!
HUH? WE SHOULD KEEP AN EYE ON HIM!
I CAN'T STAND TO WATCH THIS!!
THOOM
?!
Wah!

OW...
YOU ONLY THINK ABOUT YOURSELF!
I CAN'T TAKE THIS ANYMORE !!
SMAK
SORRY!
LET'S GO, YURI!
WHAT'RE YOU LOOKIN' AT?!
...
STAAARE
WANNA GO DRINKING? I'LL PAY!
YEAH. SOUNDS GOOD.
SHIRO BABY!
YOO-HOO!
HUH?
Hey!! Yuri!
WHAT'S IT TO YOU?! BUTT OUT!
SHE MUST REALLY LIKE YOU.
SHOULDN'T YOU GO AFTER HER?

HE'S SIMPLY ENJOYING HIS NEWFOUND FREEDOM.
THAT OLD GOAT!! AFTER BECOMING AN EXORCIST, HE REALLY CUT LOOSE!
MW AAAH
?!
HEY!
GAH!
TADOOM
BWOOMP

HE IS HANDSOME THOUGH ...
HIS PERSONALITY IS THE WORST. DON'T MIND HIM.
TNK
MY I.D. CARD!
AND MY OWN ROOM!
FLOP
GRIN

YOU'RE SO MEAN TO ME, RICK!!
...BUT I CAN'T BELIEVE JENNY DID!
Tee hee
I ALWAYS KNEW YOU'D BECOME AN EXWIRE...
LIKE ME, YOU'RE JUNIOR SECOND CLASS AND A SECOND-CLASS TAMER.
But the pay sucks!
GEH !!
You would!
OH!
WHEN I'M YOUR BOSS, I'LL RUN YOU RAGGED!!
WA
HA
HA
I'M AN EXWIRE ON THE PATH TO SUCCESS!!
INSTEAD OF DEFEATING DEMONS...
...I ENJOY STUDYING AND RAISING THEM.
CHATTER
CHATTER
SHIRO!
CONGRAT-ULATIONS!!

OH?
I WONDER WHO?
HE REMINDS ME OF SOMEONE!
HM? THAT GUY...
JUNIOR EXORCIST SECOND CLASS...
THAT IS ABEL FRANKEN, THE CURRENT PALADIN.
...YURI EGIN.
CONGRAT-ULATIONS, YURI!!
JENNY!!
RICK!!
Thanks!
KYAAAH
!!
MOM'S GETTING INDUCTED TOO?
She was in Fujimoto's class!

High rank, high level
First Class
Mid rank, low level
Second Class
ONCE A YEAR AT THE VATICAN, THOSE WHO PASS THE CERTIFICATION EXAM ARE INSTATED AS EXORCISTS.
THIS IS SOOO COOL!!
THEIR RANKS...
...DEPEND ON THE CLASS OF DEMON THEY EXORCIZED ALONE DURING THE EXAM.
AT THE CEREMONY, THE WORLD'S EXORCISTS ASSEMBLE TO SIZE UP THEIR NEW PEERS.
YOU'RE SURE TO SEE SOME FACES YOU KNOW.
HUH? WHO?!

BETWIXT LIGHT AND DARK...
...AND WITH AN INTREPID SPIRIT...
...PRACTICE SELF-RESTRAINT ...
...SERVE HUMANITY...
...AND BE FAITHFUL TO OTHERS.
IN THE NAME OF THE GRIGORI AND THE PALADINS THROUGHOUT HISTORY...
...I DUB THEE KNIGHT.
IS TH-THIS...
N...
NO WAY!
IS THIS AN EXORCIST INDUCTION CEREMONY?!

TOP OF HIS CLASS, SENIOR EXORCIST FIRST CLASS AT THE JAPAN BRANCH OF THE KNIGHTS OF THE TRUE CROSS...
Bellum Vita Mori Forum
...SHIRO FUJIMOTO!

WELL THEN...
...I'LL TAKE THESE AS MY GIFT.
IT MAY SOUND STRANGE COMING FROM ME...
...BUT I'M GLAD THAT SECTION 13...
...HAS RELEASED YOU.
WARNING
IF YOU EXPERIENCE ANY PHYSICAL ABNORMALITIES...
...DON'T HESITATE TO COME BACK.
BITE ME, BALDY!
CHATTER
CHATTER
CHATTER

YOU'RE GETTING OLDER...
...FUJIMOTO.
KOFF
KOFF
BZMP
VREEE
YOU SHOULDN'T HAVE JUST STOOD THERE!
THAT STUPID MISTAKE IS GONNA COST YOU YOUR LIFE!
HA HA...
... NGH!
GASP
AS YOUR GUARDIAN, I AT LEAST WANTED TO GIVE YOU...
GASP
...A GIFT TO CELEBRATE YOUR FINALLY BECOMING AN EXORCIST.
GASP
NOW I'LL LOOK BAD...
KOFF
TCH!
I DON'T NEED YOUR FILTHY CHARITY!
MY EYESIGHT WORSENS AND THEY IMMEDIATELY GET RID OF ME.
I SHOULD'VE JUST CRUSHED ONE EYE A LONG TIME AGO!
VERY GOOD...
HA!
GASP
GASP
THAT'S THE SPIRIT.

CHAPTER 103: SSC11:29
WHY IS HE STILL AN EXWIRE?!
EVERYONE RECOGNIZES HIS ABILITY!
I HEARD HE RECENTLY PASSED THE EXORCIST CERTIFICATION EXAM.
ISN'T IT A LITTLE LATE?
WELL, HE'S A TROUBLEMAKER AND A PROBLEM CHILD.
UH-HUH...

Blue Exorcist Chapter 102: SsC05:35

WHAT'S THAT...
...BLUE FLAME OVER THERE?
FLIKR FLIKR
IT'S A RINKA.
THAT'S ODD!
SATAN!

I HATE YOUR TYPE THE MOST.
REGROUP!
YURI! WE'RE GOING!
SO GO DIE IF YOU WANT TO.
HE'S NOT JUST PRICKLY...
FATHER FUJIMOTO...
HE'S DESTRUC-TIVE.

YEAH, BUT... NO!
EXORCISTS SAVE PEOPLE FROM DEMONS!
HAVE I HEARD THIS ARGUMENT SOMEWHERE BEFORE?
THEY DON'T KILL PERFECTLY SAFE DEMONS!
HUH?
THAT'LL GET YOU KILLED.
ARE YOU SERIOUS? BWA HA HA!
SOME DEMONS HELP US FIGHT...
SO WE HAVE TO GET ALONG!

W...
!
FSHHH
WHY...?
BECAUSE THEY'RE DEMONS.
BUT ...
...THEY WERE TERRIFIED AND FLEEING!
SO WHAT?
EXORCISTS EXORCISE DEMONS.
HUH...?

I GET IT. YOU'RE STRONG.
BUT YOU SCARED EVERYONE!
INCLUDING ME!
NEEEE!
NEEEE!
THE WAY YOU FIGHT IS DANGEROUS!
...
???
SHIRO ...?
NEEEE!
NEEEE!
NEEEE!
KCHK
BLAM
BLAM
KEEGHK!
BLAM
NEE...
TWITCH
BLAM

HOP
POINK
THE GREENMEN OF THE FOREST ARE FLEEING THE FIRE.
LET 'EM GO! THEY'RE HARMLESS!
NEE!
SWIP
TMP
TMP
NEE!
NEE!
NEE!
NEE!
NEE!
NEE!
GREENMEN ?!
SHIRO...
WOW...
...ARE YOU HURT?
UM...
SHIRO...
CHATTER
CHATTER
Whoa
Him?
Hey!

WHO
GYAAR!
R
THAT KID...
...HAS SOME MOVES!
AND HE'S STILL AN EXWIRE?!
WHAT'S HIS NAME?!
M
M
M
IS HE EVEN HUMAN?
He's about my age...
HA HA... IT'S SHIRO.
NEE!
NEE!
NEE!
NEE!
NEE!
!

BOOM
KRAKL FOOSH
THUMP
POP
KRAKL
POP
POP
POP

PING
GRAA
EE II
EE
A
W
EEE!!
G
A
A
W
SH
PEH!
DIE!
H

GRAAAAH!
BHS
H
SNAP
SWAS
KRAK
SLASH
KRAK
KRAK
...!!
HEY...IS THAT SHIRO?
IS HE CRAZY?
AN EXWIRE RUSHED IN ALONE!
SERIOUSLY ?
HUH? WHAT HAPPENED ?
NOW! BURN THEM!!
THE ROOTS HAVE STOPPED!
GASP
SILENCE
Y...
YES, SIR!!

AGH!
HRNGH?
WHO IS THAT?
STOP!!
GROOOAAR!
BO
OSH
HUP
FOO
SH
GRIP
GRAB
SWIP
CLASH

GW
BURN THE ROOTS AND ADVANCE WITH CAUTION!!
GRRR!
GRRR
AAA
WH
AM
KYAH!
GYAH!
DON'T GET TOO CLOSE TO THE ROOTS!!
THUD
WHAM
WAH!
POOM
SPS
HH
HNGH ?!
?!
?!
WHAT-
YOU KLUTZ!
TCH!
WUD
GAH!
UMPH
CLIC
GRENADE: HOLY WATER
FWISH

GRROOO
GRAA!
GRRR
GRRR
GRRR
TH-THAT'S THE ENT!
YIKES!
IT'S HUGE!
ATTACK!

...YOU BRAT!
DON'T TALK TO ME...
TCH!
?!
HE REALLY EXISTS, HUH?
IS THAT SHIRO?
That handsome guy??
WHO'S THAT?
WHAT'S GOING ON?
... REMEMBER ME?
D-DON'T YOU...
ALL RIGHT...
...TAKE YOUR POSITIONS, PAGES!
IT'S BIG, SO DON'T GET CLOSE UNTIL IT'S WEAK!
...THEN STRIKE THE HEART IN ITS HEAD!!
DAMAGE ITS ROOTS TO WEAKEN IT...

BLUSH
YOU!
?!
WHSH
REMEMBER ME? I'M YURI!
...
YOU LOOK WELL!
HUFF
HUFF
IT'S BEEN FIVE YEARS!
HUFF
I'M SO HAPPY!!
HUFF

CHATTER
CHATTER
CHATTER
SHIRO!

AS EXORCISTS AND EXWIRES PERFORM THE EXORCISM, PAGES WILL LEND BACKUP.
WE WILL SURROUND THE ENT WITH TORCHES TO WEAKEN IT.
HAND OUT THE TORCHES!
THERE'S MOM!
HAS SHE GROWN SINCE LAST TIME? MAYBE A LITTLE?
WHAT DID YOU SAY?!
YURI'S AN EXCELLENT STUDENT.
I'M MORE WORRIED ABOUT YOU, JENNY!
DON'T GET IN THE WAY, YURI!
THIS IS MY FIRST REAL FIGHT!!
OKAY!
I HOPE I DON'T MAKE A DUMB MISTAKE!
PAT PAT
THEN I'LL BE NICE TO YOU, OKAY?
YOU'RE ONLY NICE TO YURI!
GRARR!
WHOA
AND THE EXWIRES!
THE EXORCISTS HAVE ARRIVED!

UH-OH...
WHERE AM I?
FOR TODAY'S MISSION, WE WILL EXORCISE AN ENT!
MISSION ?!
GATHER ROUND!
?!
SOME TOURISTS AND HIKERS FUSED WITH AN EVIL GHOST AND TURNED UP DEAD!
IT IS A HIGHLY DANGEROUS DEMON!!
YOU WILL BE IN A SUPPORTING ROLE, BUT STAY SHARP!!
YES, SIR!!
YES, SIR!!
HM?
I CAN'T HEAR YOU!!

...IT'S AWFUL!!
ANYWAY ...
YEAH ...
HM?
AFTER ALL, I'M A DEMON.
I CAN'T SAY I UNDERSTAND HOW YOU FEEL.
I DON'T GET IT!
YOU CREEP!
I CAN'T STAND IT!!
LEAVING ALREADY?
IT'S TOO MUCH!
Stay together!
Stop playing around!
WHAT A HORRIBLE WAY TO GROW UP.
I DIDN'T WANT TO SEE THAT.

I'M GONNA SURVIVE THIS...
...AND GET OUT OF HERE!!
HUFF
HUFF
THIS IS THE PLACE THAT GAVE BIRTH TO THE MAN KNOWN AS SHIRO FUJIMOTO.
WASN'T THERE ANY OTHER WAY?
I MEAN...
...IT JUST ISN'T RIGHT!!
IS THIS THE ONLY WAY TO DEFEND THE WORLD?!

...
AGH...
THEIR TREATMENT WAS INHUMANE.
THEY WERE TESTED AND DIED LIKE GUINEA PIGS.
HUFF
HUFF
HUFF
GASP
...
HEH!
HEY...
...GORO.
YOU'RE STILL ALIVE? HOW HAVE YOU BEEN?
M...
THOSE LUCKY ENOUGH TO SURVIVE LOST THEIR HUMANITY.
MAWAWAWAWAWA

AT FIRST...
THEN DR. EMINESCU...
...WE MADE COUNTLESS CLONES TO SERVE AS NEW VESSELS FOR HIM. HOWEVER, IT DIDN'T GO WELL.
...SUGGESTED DEVELOPING AN ELIXIR FOR PROVIDING IMMORTALITY.
WITH SUCH AN ELIXIR, HE COULD USE ANY BODY AS A VESSEL.
HOWEVER...
...TESTING THE DRUGS WAS HELL ON THE CLONES.

IT'S BEEN FOUR YEARS, BUT HE'S STILL A SUBJECT AT SECTION 13.
HEH HEH!
JUST DIE, WOULD YA?
LUCIFER WILL NOT GIVE UP...
...UNTIL HE ACHIEVES THE PERFECT BODY.
THE TEST SUBJECTS...
...EXIST TO SUPPRESS HIS INSANITY.

FATHER FUJIMOTO!!!
HE'S REALLY GROWN!!
?!!
TMP
TMP
I HEAR YOU'RE AN EXCELLENT EXWIRE.
I HOPE YOU MAKE EXORCIST SOON!
GOOD WORK.
THIS WAS YOUR ANNUAL DAY FOR EXPERIMENTATION.

...!
HUFF
HUFF
LUCIFER...
I SAW HIM ONCE BEFORE, BUT...
THIS TIME, HE WAS MUCH MORE...
DID YOU SENSE...
...HOW DISASTROUS HIS UNRESTRAINED WRATH WOULD BE?
I GET IT NOW.
HM?
THAT'S WHY.
SHIRO.

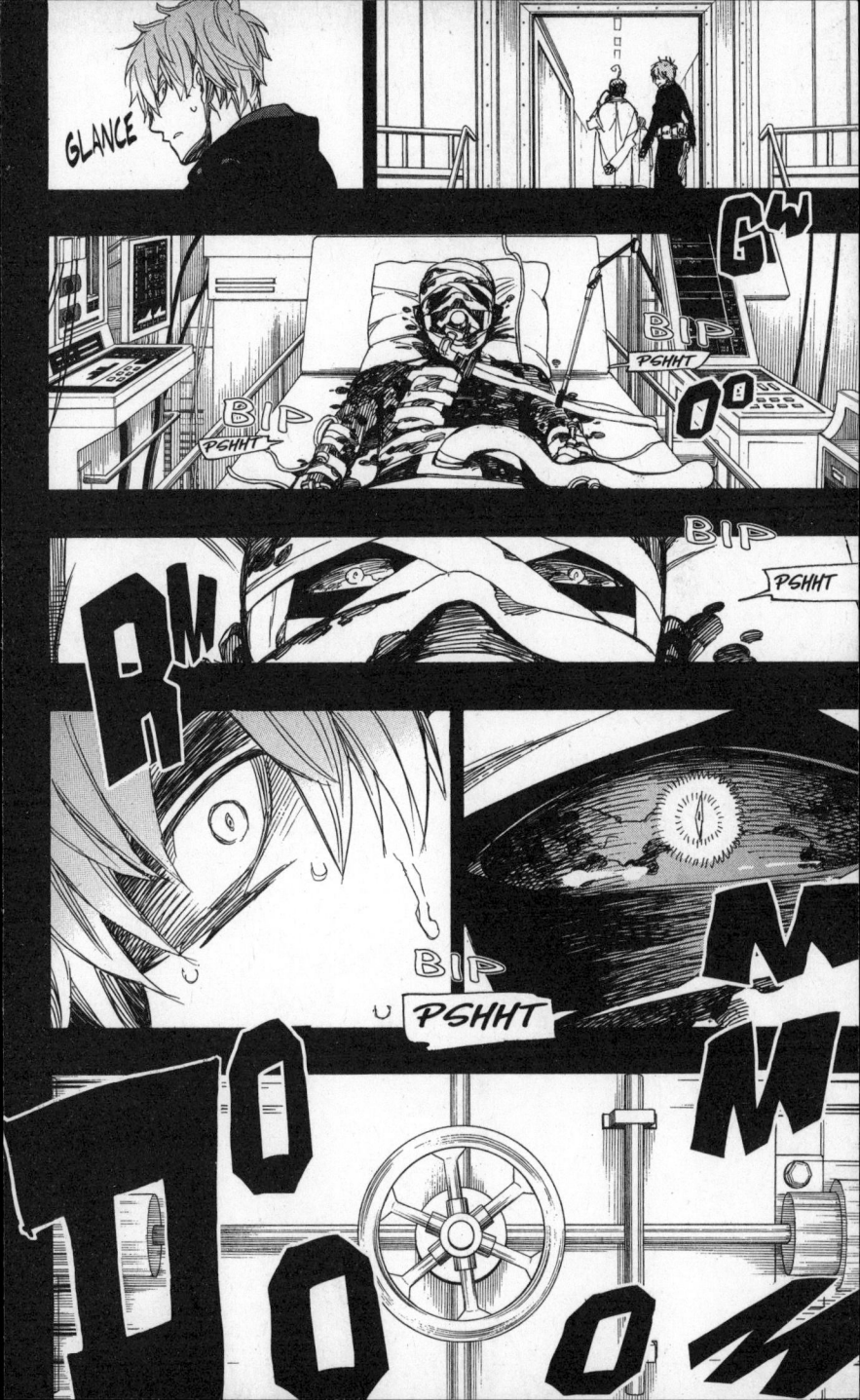
GLANCE
BIP
PSHHT
BIP
PSHHT
BIP
PSHHT
BIP
PSHHT

GW
WHEEZ
WHEEZ
I... KOFF
...BELIEVE THAT!
FWO
OPA
TCH!
CONTINUING THE EXPERIMENT IS DANGEROUS.
THAT'S ENOUGH FOR TODAY.
IT'S UNFORTUNATE, BUT I STILL EXPECT SUCCESS WITH THE ELIXIRS, MR. EMINESCU.
MY APOLOGIES.

BEEP
WHEEZ
KOFF
HAAH
SPLORT
BEEP
KOFF
YOU CAN ACQUIRE A NEW BODY LATER.
LEAVE ASSIAH ALONE AND QUIETLY RETURN TO GEHENNA.
BEEP
IF YOU ABANDON THAT BODY, YOU WILL BE FREE OF YOUR SUFFERING.
BEEP
LUCIFER...
BEEP
KOFF
...!
HAH!
BIP
...SO...
...CRUEL.
KOFF KOFF KOFF
GASP
...ARE...
YOU...
KOFF
BEEP
BEEP
GASP
SAMAEL ...
BIP
...I...
...WILL BE...
...REWARDED.
BIP
GASP
SOMEDAY...
BIP

BIP
BIP
BIP
CAN YOU HEAR MY VOICE, BIG BROTHER?
BIP
PSHHT
HOW DO YOU FEEL?
GAHGK!
BIP
...
KOFF KOFF
KOFF
KOFF
KOFF KOFF
KOFF
THE ELIXIR APPEARS TO HAVE *FAILED.*

BIP
PSHHT
GLURGL
WE BELIEVE THIS DRUG WILL ALLEVIATE LORD LUCIFER'S SUFFERING.
PSHHT
...ALL THAT CRUEL EXPERIMENTATION WAS TO CREATE A DRUG?
SPIN
SPIN
SPIN
AND IT WAS ALL FOR LUCIFER'S BODY??
...IN OTHER WORDS...
UM...
HEH
STAY HERE.
TAK
TAK
BUSTLE
UM...
...IS THERE ANY CHANGE IN HIS VITAL SIGNS?
BUSTLE
BIP
N-NO! NO CHANGE!
BIP
WHY?
THIRTY MINUTES HAVE PASSED.
WHAT IS HIS STATUS, MR. EMINESCU?

...AND INJECTED IT INTO DEAD MICE AND HUMAN FLESH.
FIRST, WE DREW BLOOD FROM 59 DEMONS WITH SUPERB PHYSICAL REGENERATION...
ALLOW ME TO EXPLAIN!
THIS IS ELIXIR 51!
E-51
ELEVEN SUBJECTS DEMONSTRATED HEIGHTENED CELLULAR REGENERATION.
THEN WE DREW BLOOD FROM SAMPLES EXHIBITING ARRESTED NECROSIS AND APPLIED IT TO THE ENTIRE LUCIFER GROUP.
...WE EXTRACTED CELLS FOR REFINEMENT, AND THIS WAS THE RESULT!
FROM THOSE 11 SUBJECTS...

IT'S SHEMIHAZA...
...AND EVERYONE FROM THE GRIGORI AGENCY.
THEN YOU MAY PROCEED.
WE'RE BEGINNING THE EXPERIMENT!
!
OH MY!
*ANOTHER NAME FOR THE GRIGORI.
WE CANNOT LEAVE A SACRED SAGE* ALONE.
I MUST WITNESS EVERYTHING.
YOUR ATTENTION, PLEASE.

SIR PHELES...
MY APOLOGIES FOR BEING LATE.
BIP
ARE YOU READY TO BEGIN THE EXPERIMENT...
...MR. EMINESCU?
BIP
YES.
KOFF
KOFF
KOFF
BIP
HE'S IN EXTREMELY POOR CONDITION TODAY...
BIP
Koff
Koff
WHEEZ
...WHICH IS PERFECT FOR THE EXPERIMENT.
BIP
WHEEZ

BIP
BIP
BIP
BIP
BIP
PSHHT
BIP
PSHHT

CHAPTER 102: SsC05:35
FROM HERE ON...
...STAND WITH YOUR FEET SHOULDER WIDTH APART AND CLASP YOUR HANDS BEHIND YOUR BACK. STAY BEHIND ME, AND DON'T TALK.

Oh dear...
There are provisions in the pouches around your waist.
Seriously?!

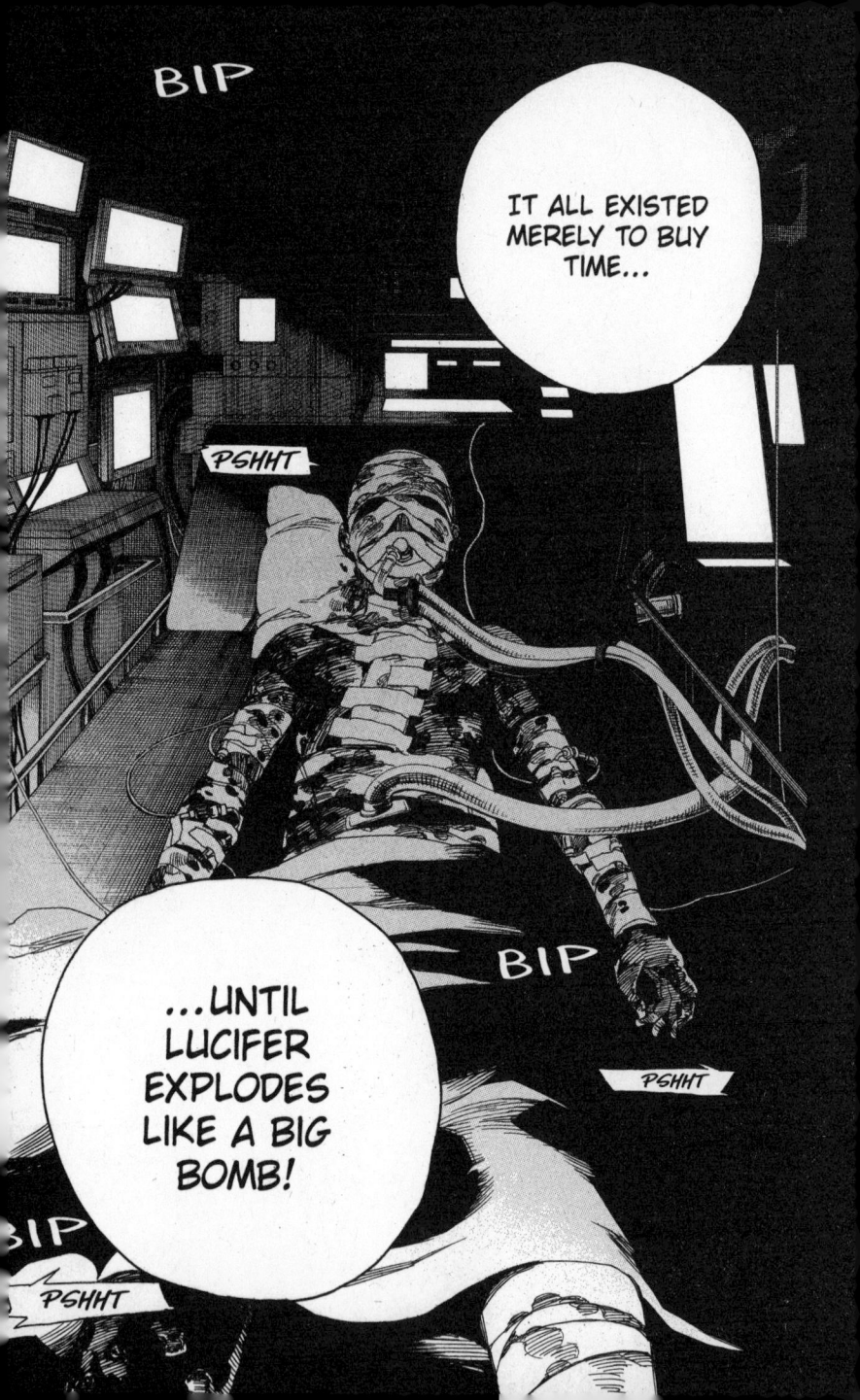
BIP
IT ALL EXISTED MERELY TO BUY TIME...
PSHHT
BIP
PSHHT
...UNTIL LUCIFER EXPLODES LIKE A BIG BOMB!
BIP
PSHHT

IT'S ALL FOR *LUCIFER!*
THE SUBJECTS AND RESEARCHERS ...
...AND THE RESEARCH...
...AND *EVERYTHING* AT THIS FACILITY...

"...SPENT COUNTLESS LIVES IN EXPERIMENTS TO CREATE VESSELS FOR DEMONS."
"FATHER FUJIMOTO..."
"...WAS ONE OF THE SUBJECTS THOSE EXPERIMENTS CREATED."
SO YOU ARE THE ENEMY!
BUT WHY DO ALL THIS?!

THAT'S RIGHT...
SHIRO FUJIMOTO WAS BORN HERE.
HE WAS A CLONE OF AZAZEL, KING OF SPIRITS.
"MEPHISTO..."

...THEY WERE TRYING TO CREATE VESSELS CAPABLE OF HOUSING DEMON KINGS.
ITS AREAS OF STUDY WERE COMPLEX...
...SO YOU WOULDN'T UNDERSTAND.
UH, YEAH, BUT...
SECTION 13 CLONED DEMON KINGS AND CULTIVATED THEM FOR POSSESSION.
SIMPLY PUT...

WHY?
HOW SHOULD I KNOW?
BECAUSE IT WAS A PLACE OF HORROR.
ASYLUM SERVED AS A FRONT FOR THE RESEARCH FACILITY HIDDEN UNDERNEATH AND KNOWN AS SECTION 13.
RESEARCH?
KRII

THE SCHOOL TOOK IN ORPHANS...
...WITH TEMPTAINT OR DEMON BLOOD...
TMP
TMP
TMP
GOOD MORNING, SIR PHELES.
GOOD MORNING.
TMP
TMP
PRETEND LIKE YOU'RE MY BODYGUARD.
...AND TRAINED THEM TO BE EXORCISTS.
TMP
TMP
TMP
DO YOU KNOW WHY?
IT WAS DISMANTLED AFTER THE BLUE NIGHT.
OH!
THAT WAS MOM...

SMOOTH
YOU'RE LATE, OKUMURA.
COME WITH ME.
?!
MEPHISTO'S OFFICE AGAIN??
KACHAK
HUH?
!
SABINUKI
THAT'S QUITE A JUMP!
FOUR.
HOW MANY YEARS HAVE PASSED?
FOR MANY YEARS, ASYLUM WAS A CHILDREN'S SHELTER...
...AS WELL AS AN EXORCIST TRAINING SCHOOL.

YOU'RE LIKE A NOSY HOUSEKEEPER, BUT I APPRECIATE YOUR DISCRETION. ☆
OKUMURA?
AGH!
SLAM
HEH HEH HEH...
OH DEAR...
...
THE CRAM SCHOOL IS CALLED ASYLUM NOW...
...BUT IS THAT THE SAME THING AS SECTION 13?
WHAT'S THIS "SECTION 13" HE WAS TALKING ABOUT?
YOU WON'T JUST TELL ME?
KEEP GOING AND FIND OUT.

IF YOU EVER YIELD TO A DEMON, EVEN ONCE...
...YOU HAVE TO GRANT ME ONE FAVOR. ANYTHING I ASK!
HUH?
WHAT-EVER.
I ACCEPT.
004
SO KEEP YOUR PROMISE!!

SOUNDS FUN.
VERY WELL THEN!
I'LL RECOMMEND YOU FOR EXWIRE.
HUH ?!
SERIOUSLY ?!
FATHER FUJIMOTO!
HE'S REALLY FEISTY.
REMINDS ME OF MYSELF AGAIN...
...BUT HE'S ALSO TOTALLY DIFFERENT!
?!
HOWEVER ...
...THERE IS ONE CONDITION.

I'M GONNA KILL EVERY DEMON I SEE...
...AND KILL, AND KILL, UNTIL I'M PALADIN...
...AND WHEN MY OWNERS ARE FINALLY DONE USING ME...
...I'M GONNA TEAR OUT YOUR THROAT WITH MY TEETH!

BECOMING PALADIN ISN'T A TICKET TO FREEDOM.
DRILL THIS INTO YOUR HEAD.
WHEN YOU BECOME AN EXWIRE...
...YOU SIGN A CONTRACT OF MORINATH FORBIDDING YOU FROM LEAKING INFORMATION ABOUT SECTION 13—AND YOUR *LIFE* IS THE COLLATERAL!
HEH HEH HEH!
THE TRAINING IS GRUELING...
...AND FORMER TEST SUBJECTS NEVER LEAVE THE ORGANIZATION ALIVE!
EVEN IF YOU MAKE PALADIN...
...YOU'LL SWEAR FEALTY TO THE ORDER AND BE ITS *DOG!*
HA HA HA!
YOU WILL *NEVER* BE FREE!
THEN BRING IT ON.

GR
YOU CREATED ME TO SAVE PEOPLE FROM DEMONS...
GRNCH GRNCH
...BUT NO THANKS!
I'M NOT GOING OUT AS SOME DEMONIC SACRIFICE!!
HUFF
HUFF
ENORT
HUFF
...
HEE ...
... HEE HEE!
HOO HOO HA HA HA!
YOU'RE SO IGNORANT AND STUPID!

AS AN EXWIRE...
...I'LL ONLY HAVE TO BE IN EXPERIMENTS ONCE A YEAR!
AND WHEN I'M AN EXORCIST...
...I GET TO LIVE ON MY OWN!!
AND WHEN I'M PALADIN...
...I'LL BE ROLLING IN STATUS, MONEY, HONOR AND BIG BOO- I MEAN, WOMEN!
I'LL BE FREE!!

...MAKE ME AN EXWIRE!
EVERY 15 YEARS, EACH TEST GROUP RAISES AN EXWIRE!
SHAKE
FATHER FUJIMOTO !!!
AND THIS IS THE YEAR! GROUP AZ HASN'T CHOSEN YET...
...SO CHOOSE ME!!
...AND I FIT THE CRITERIA...

I SEE...
HUH?
SO NOW WHAT?
YOU GONNA KILL ME?
AREN'T YOU THE DIRECTOR OF SECTION 13...
...MEPHISTO PHELES?
WAH HA HA HA !!
HYA HA HA
BAM
BAM
BAM
...
YOU CRACK ME UP!
WEE HEE HEE!!
YOU... SNORT ...
...REALLY ARE INTRIGUING!
OH...?
YOU LIKE ME, HUH?
IN THAT CASE...

...THE WORLD'S A TRASH HEAP.
YEAH...
THE WORLD IS A HARSH PLACE.
WOULDN'T IT BE EASIER JUST TO GET ALONG QUIETLY HERE?
BUT IT'S BETTER THAN SECTION 13!
...I WAS GONNA ESCAPE HERE, AND GO FAR AWAY, AND BE FREE!
WHEN I SAVED UP ENOUGH MONEY...
INSTEAD OF LIVING IN ISOLATION WITH A BUNCH OF GUYS WHO LOOK LIKE ME...
...I'D RATHER DIE!

COME CLOSER.
I HEAR...
...YOU OFTEN SLIP PAST THE GUARDS TO ESCAPE SECTION 13.
Heh heh heh!
INTRIGUING ...
AND YOU EVEN HAD A REFUGE IN THE SLUMS.
YOU'RE THE FIRST SUBJECT TO DO THAT.
TCH
I DIDN'T STEAL IT!
I SOLD PARTS AND DID ODD JOBS LIKE CLEANING...
...AND JUST SAVED UP.
THEY FOUND 30,000 YEN IN YOUR HIDEOUT.
!
HOW DID YOU COME BY IT?
THAT MUST HAVE BEEN DIFFICULT.
YOU'RE JUST A CHILD.

SNEAK
PARDON THE INTRUSION.
I'VE BROUGHT THE SUBJECT YOU REQUESTED.
THANK YOU.
YOU MAY GO NOW.
YES, SIR!
SO...YOU'RE SHIRO, EXPERIMENTAL SUBJECT NUMBER AO-004...
...IN THE AZAZEL GROUP!
...

TNK
GOOD LUCK, MOM!
THIS PLACE IS LIKE THE MILITARY...
...BUT SHE SEEMS TO HAVE CALMED DOWN.
ENTER.
I RECOGNIZE THIS PLACE...
HM?
KLICK
KRII

I'M AN OLD HAND! AND I'M ROOM CHIEF!
IF YOU HAVE QUESTIONS, JUST ASK ME!
EKKS... WAWAH?
AND I HEAR THE PAY'S A LOT BETTER!
EXWIRE! THEN YOU GET YOUR OWN ROOM!
THANKS...
...
SO GOOD LUCK!
GIRLS GET IN EASY.
UM...
YUKIOTOKO ?
...SHIRO.
I THINK HIS NAME IS...
HE'S LIKE THE YUKIOTOKO!
...HAVE YOU SEEN A MEAN BOY WITH WHITE HAIR AROUND?
OH...
DUNNO. I DON'T RECALL THE NAME.

ARE YOU CRAZY?
MOST KIDS CRY THEIR FIRST NIGHT.
WHAT'RE YOU GIGGLING ABOUT?
IT'S BUGGING ME, SO I CAN'T SLEEP!
SORRY.
OH.
HUH?
BECAUSE TRAINING IS HARD!
WHY DO THEY CRY?
WHAT?!
HA HA! THAT'S GOOD!
ACTUALLY...
...I ENJOYED STUDYING DEMONS!
IF YOU DO REALLY WELL, YOU'LL BECOME AN EXWIRE AND JOIN THE ELITE COURSE!
WHEN YOU'RE AN EXORCIST, YOU GET TO WORK AND BE FREE!

YES, THAT IS OUR OBJECTIVE.

OKU AND OBABA WERE EXORCISTS.
IF I BECOME ONE TOO...
...OKU WILL BE ANGRY.

QUIET DOWN THERE!
BAM
!

HEE HEE
AND NIKO-
BUT OBABA WILL BE HAPPY!
HEE HEE

AFTER SUPPER, YOU TRAIN UNTIL 10 P.M.
LIGHTS OUT AT 11 P.M.
LEAVING THE FACILITY IS PROHIBITED.
"SHE NEEDS TO START SCHOOL SOON."
IS THIS A... SCHOOL?
YOU MAY THINK OF IT THAT WAY.
AM I GONNA BE AN EXORCIST?

AFTER ROLL CALL, YOU WILL CLEAN THE DORM.
AFTER BREAKFAST, FROM 8 A.M. TO 2 P.M., YOU HAVE GENERAL EDUCATION.
FROM 2 P.M. TO 5 P.M....
...YOU STUDY AND TRAIN TO BECOME EXORCISTS.

IT IS A FACILITY THAT SHELTERS AND EDUCATES CHILDREN LIKE YOU WHO HAVE A CERTAIN *APTITUDE.*
APTI... TUDE?
WHAT'S THAT?
QUESTIONS ?
UM...
...WHAT KIND OF PLACE IS THIS?
THE POTENTIAL TO BE AN *EXORCIST.*
EXOR...CIST?
YOU WILL GET UP AT 6 A.M.

Someone, please take care of Yuri. I can't do it because I'm sick and can't move. I have no one to rely
Please, be mother to
love her.
Yoko
THIS OLD LETTER WAS SEWN...
...INTO THE LINING OF YOUR BAG.
OH...I AM?
RUSTLE
?
?
???
?
I... CAN'T READ...
YOUR FATHER IS UNKNOWN.
YOKO EGIN'S MOTHER AND FATHER, YOUR GRANDPARENTS, COMMITTED SUICIDE.
WHEN THE EGIN FAMILY'S BUSINESS CONGLOMERATE DISSOLVED, THE FAMILY FELL TO RUIN...
...AND ITS MEMBERS SCATTERED.
YOU ARE ALONE AND HELPLESS.
THEREFORE, ASYLUM WILL OFFICIALLY ACCEPT YOU.
ANY QUESTIONS?

YOU COME THIS WAY.
NO DAWDLING!
WHERE ARE YOU TAKING HIM?
HEY!
WE HAVE INVESTIGATED YOUR BACKGROUND.
YOUR NAME IS *YURI EGIN.*
YOU ARE THE CHILD OF *YOKO EGIN,* WHO DIED SIX YEARS AGO.

WHAT IS YOUR NAME, GIRL?
HUH?
UM... YURI.
...
AND YOUR LAST NAME?
WE'LL TAKE THEM FROM HERE.
THESE ARE THE CHILDREN I TOLD YOU ABOUT EARLIER THAT WE WANT YOU TO PROTECT.
SHIRO, YOU COME WITH ME.
NEVER MIND. COME WITH ME, MISS YURI.
...
YOU'RE TOO FILTHY FOR A BED.
FIRST, YOU NEED TO CLEAN YOURSELF UP.
WHP

IS THIS ASYLUM?
IT'S KINDA DARK.
THIS IS THE EXORCISM CRAM SCHOOL!
WAS IT CALLED ASYLUM 40 YEARS AGO?
RUSTLE
PEEK
GOOD WORK.
...

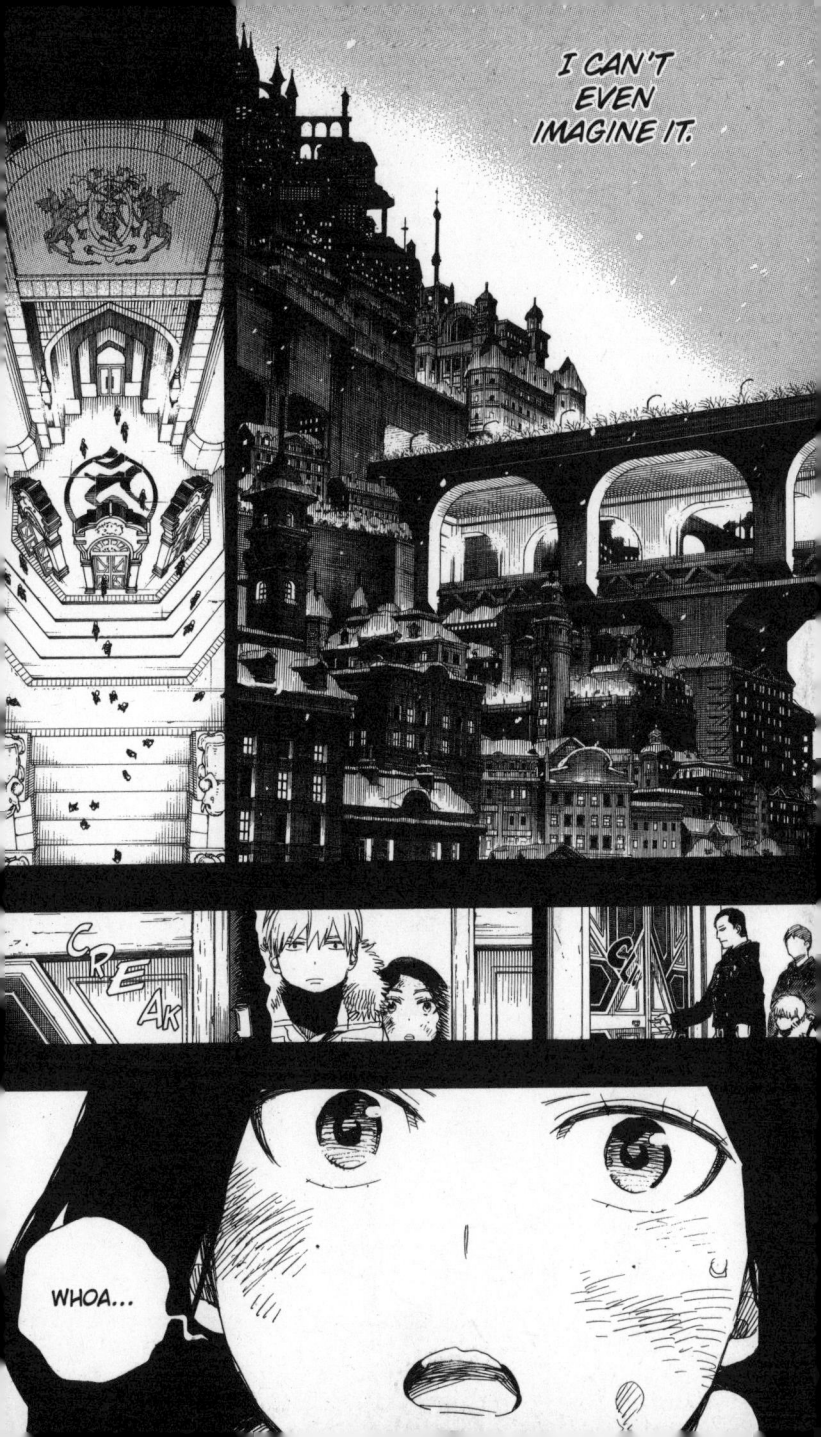
I CAN'T EVEN IMAGINE IT.
CREAK
WHOA...

...SO...
I NEVER KNEW REAL LONELINESS...
...I DON'T KNOW HOW LONELY OR HOPELESS...
GRIP
...MY MOTHER FEELS RIGHT NOW.

BUT I HAD YUKIO.
...PROVIDED A HOME FOR ME.
AND FATHER FUJIMOTO...
SO I WAS TRULY FORTUNATE.

CHAPTER 101: SsC04:36

Blue Exorcist Chapter 100: SSC00:40

WOW...
正十字学園
Seijuudi gakuen

VROOM
問店
IS IT NICE?
WHAT'S THAT PLACE LIKE?
ASYLUM?
NO, IT'S HORRIBLE.
YOU'VE GOT ROTTEN LUCK, KID.

GRRRRRRR
HEY, UH...
...DOGGY?
!!
SHE'S AN ORPHAN, SO SHE WON'T TELL ANYONE.
ANYWAY, SHE HEARD US.
BUT WE STILL HAVEN'T–
GRR
??
YOU CAN SEE THIS BLACK DOG?
ALL RIGHT...
YES, SIR!
...COME WITH ME, GIRL.
TAKE HER BACK TO ASYLUM AND CHECK HER OUT.
IF SHE CAN SEE DEMONS, *THAT* CHANGES EVERYTHING.

WE'VE FOUND YOU!
ALL RIGHT, FINE.
DON'T BOTHER RESISTING, SHIRO!
...?!
GRRRR
RUFF
...
YOU'RE THE ONLY ONE FROM THE AZAZEL GROUP TO DO THIS.
IS THIS WHERE YOU'VE BEEN SINCE YOU SLIPPED AWAY?
NICE HIDEOUT YOU GOT HERE.
ROWF
ROWF
I DUNNO. JUST SOME HOMELESS KID WHO SNUCK IN.
!!
WHO'S THE GIRL?
AND-
GRRR
GRFF

SIGH
MOM SORTA REMINDS ME OF SHIEMI SOMETIMES.
THAT'S... THAT'S WEIRD...
...
YUKIO.
"EVEN THE YUKIOTOKO IS WARM!"
KRA
UH-OH!
WAH!
WALK SOFTLY!
WE HAVE TO CATCH HIM!
!!
HUFF
HUFF
HUFF
HUFF

YOU ARE WARM!
EVEN THE YUKIOTOKO IS WARM!

HUG
UGH...
...IT'S FREEZING!
FWP
WHAT'RE YOU DOING?!
DIDN'T YOU KNOW IT'S WARMER CLOSE TOGETHER?
Ask first!
BUT MAYBE THE YUKIOTOKO ISN'T WARM?
I'M NOT THE YUKIOTOKO!
What the...?! Seriously?!
...
OR MAYBE I AM...
AFTER ALL, I'M NOT HUMAN.
KRAK!
OH!

FINE.
TCH...

SO HOW ABOUT IT?
...
YOU WANTED A BENEFIT, RIGHT?
FWP
FWP
FWP
FWP

AND THEY BETTER HAVE SOME MAJOR GAZONGAS!
GAZONGAS?
YOU CAN STAY UNTIL MORNING.
THEN YOU CAN TAKE ME THERE.

BOOF

Shame on him!
FATHER FUJIMOTO...
...WAS ALREADY INTO BIG BOOBS BACK THEN?

?!
RUSTLE RUSTLE
HM? WHERE'D MEPHISTO GO?
I DIDN'T KNOW HE WAS SO POOR.

GYAAH!
!!!!
SAW I'VE GOT DIRTY MAGAZINES, SO...
SHUT UP ABOUT IT!!!
YOU LIKE THAT STUFF, RIGHT?
DON'T LOOK AT THAT!!!
SWITCH
WHEN THE SNOW STOPS IN THE MORNING, I'LL TAKE YOU...
?!
I KNOW A PLACE WHERE THERE'S A BUNCH OF OLD DIRTY MAGS!
...SO LET ME STAY HERE!

HUH?!
OBABA SAYS...
...HE'S PURE WHITE AND SUPER TALL AND COLD AND TERRIFYING!
...THE YUKIOTOKO !!!
Y...
Y...
YOU'RE...
...BUT YOU'RE TOO MEAN!!!!
YOU COULD LET ME STAY UNTIL THE SNOW STOPS...
JUST LIKE YOU!!
WHAT'S IN IT FOR YOU?
!
I CAN'T HAVE OTHER PEOPLE HANGING AROUND!
I BUILT THIS PLACE TO BE A HIDING PLACE!
BUT WHAT'S IN IT FOR ME?

WHADDO I CARE?!
DON'T EXPECT ANY SYMPATHY FROM ME!
GET OUT BEFORE I KILL YOU!
I'M SORRY...
I'M YURI. MY WHOLE FAMILY DIED, SO...
...I DON'T HAVE ANYWHERE TO GO.
GAH!
YOU ATE A WHOLE BAG!
TCH...
...IT'S COLD OUTSIDE, AND I'LL DIE.
BUT...
!!
I COULDN'T CARE LESS!
SO DIE.

YOU...
WHAT'RE YOU DOING IN MY HIDEOUT?!
I'LL KILL YOU!
HW
FATHER FUJIMOTO?
IT REALLY LOOKS LIKE HIM!
?
WHSH

I'M GLAD SHE GOT OUT OF THE SNOW...
...BUT THIS IS SOME GUY'S SHED! WILL SHE BE ALL RIGHT?
I BETTER KEEP AN EYE ON HER!
YOU REALLY MUSTN'T HELP TOO MUCH.
CLOMP CLOMP CLOMP
!!
WHA?
POP
!
KRINK
KR!
KR!
KR!

I can barely see, but I know they're dirty!
NIKO SAYS THESE ARE "DIRTY" MAGAZINES...
AND DIFFICULT BOOKS...
YAMADA INTERNAL SCIENCE
WITH A BED!
FOMP
RRIP
GROW...
GURGLE...
GROW...
GURRR...
OOH!
SORRY!
MUNCH MUNCH
CRNCH
CRNCH
CRNCH
SORRY...
...
FOMP
AHH...
NOD NOD

HWOOO
IF YOU AIN'T GOT MONEY, THEN GET LOST!
SLOSH
I AIN'T RUNNIN' A CHARITY!
KREAK
UMF!
STAGGER
HUFF HUFF
SOMEONE LIVES HERE!

JUST LEAVE HER.
YUCK! WHAT A CREEPY KID!

BRR BRR BRR
YOU SHOULDN'T HELP HER.
TUG
COME ON.
THIS IS AWFUL!

KLANG
Welcome!

餃子
SHOO! SHOO! PISS OFF!
FILTHY BRAT!
UM, CAN I HAVE SOME RICE?

SNIFF SNIFF SNIFF

GRRGL
I'M HUNGRY...

OKUUU!!
I HEARD THEY FOUND THREE CHARRED BODIES.
THOSE HOMELESS PEOPLE MUST'VE LEFT A FIRE GOING...
I WISH THEY WOULDN'T DO THAT!

GWO
KLANG KLANG KLANG
FIRE!!
?!
IT'S HOT!
WHAT'S GOING ON?!
IS THIS THE FACTORY WHERE MOM LIVED?
O...
OUTTA THE WAY! MOVE ASIDE!!
FIRE TRUCKS ARE COOL!
WEEE
WEEE
IT'S LIKE A BIG, WARM BONFIRE!
BURN! BURN!!
HA HA HA!
STAY BACK!
DON'T GET IN THE WAY!
SHUU
NO ...!
OKU! NIKO!
OBABA !!

BUT THIS WAS PROBABLY HIS FIRST INTELLIGENT INTERACTION.
SO I DON'T KNOW IF HE KNEW HE WAS PLAYING OR NOT.
SATAN DIDN'T HAVE AN EGO YET.
PSST
PSST
BYE-BYE!
PLAYING HOUSE.
WHAT WERE YOU DOING?
OKAAAY...
!
YURI!
YOU SHOULDN'T PLAY HERE! IT'S DANGEROUS!
LET'S MOVE FORWARD AGAIN...
BUT THERE'S SO MUCH FUN STUFF HERE!
FWSH
IF ALL THAT JUNK COLLAPSED, IT WOULD BURY YOU ALIVE.

FWOOSH
KYAH!
CLAP CLAP
HOW ABOUT THIS?
UMF!
IS HE PLAYING?
YEP.
KLINK KLANK KLONK
AH HA HA!!

WHAT'S SHE DOING?
Mom...
HOW ABOUT THIS?
THERE!
TMP
BACK THEN, RINKA WAS ONE WORD FOR SATAN.
RUSTLE RUSTLE
SATAN WOULD APPEAR IN ASSIAH FOR NO APPARENT REASON AND THEN DISAPPEAR AGAIN.
...
WAH!!
FWSH
SMAK
COOL!

KLANK
KYAH!
AND NOW-
!
CLINK
IT'S HERE...
CLINK
RINKA?
...
IT'S SATAN.
IT'S THE BLUE FLAME.
WHAT ?!

IT'S THE NEXT DAY.
HOW MUCH TIME HAS PASSED?
SHE'S STILL SMALL.
...LET'S PLAY HOUSE!
TODAY...
"WELCOME TO OUR HOUSE!"
"HELLO!"
"KNOCK! KNOCK!"
"GLUP, GLUP, GLUP, GLUP!"
"HERE YOU GO!"
"OH, DON'T MIND ME!"
"I JUST MADE COFFEE."
"WAIT RIGHT HERE."
ISN'T THAT JUST HOW LITTLE KIDS ARE?
SHE SHOULD GET SOME FRIENDS!
MAN ...
...THIS IS SO SAD.

NO.
IT TOOK ALL OF US TO RAISE HER.
...BEING TOGETHER IS MORE FUN.
BESIDES ...
...
YEAH, THAT'S RIGHT!
AH HA HA
AT THIS RATE, SHE'LL END UP LIKE OBABA.
BUT I'LL LOOK INTO IT.
LET'S MOVE FORWARD IN TIME...
I'M GLAD!
THEY SEEM HAPPY!
SHH!
THERE SHE IS!
HUH?
?!
THERE'S JUNK EVERY-WHERE!
KACHAK

SHE'S GROWING UP SO FAST!
OKU, SHE WAS JUST A NEWBORN BABE WHEN YOU FOUND HER LYING IN THE JUNKYARD AND BROUGHT HER BACK.
YEAH...
SHE NEEDS TO START SCHOOL SOON.
THE DEMON'S PANCAKES
I WOULD IF MY EYES WERE BETTER, BUT...
...
EVER THINK ABOUT WORKING AGAIN?
OKU, YOU STILL HAVE YOUR EXORCIST'S LICENSE, DON'T YOU?
...AND LIVE ON YOUR OWN!
YOU TWO COULD RENT A HOUSE...

DEMON-FIRE, AZUL, IRRLICHT, WILL-O'-THE-WISP, *IGNIS FATUUS*... IT HAS MANY NAMES.
IT'S A SPECTRAL FLAME SEEN ALL OVER THE WORLD.
A RINKA?
SLURP
PUFF PUFF
WHAT *IS* IT?

...WHILE OTHERS SAY THEY'RE GOBLINS AND FAIRIES AND THE TEMPORARY FORMS OF SACRED FOXES.
YIKES ...
NO ONE KNOWS.
HEH HEH
SOME SAY DEAD SOULS, OTHERS SAY THE FIRES OF HELL...
REALLY ?!

STOP THAT! YOU'LL TURN HER INTO A WEIRDO LIKE YOU!
OBABA!
SO I CAN BE FRIENDS WITH THEM!
AWESOME!
I HOPE THEY'RE FAIRIES OR FOXES!
WEIRDOS HAVE MORE FUN!
HAW HAW HAW

OKU AND OBABA USED TO BE EXORCISTS.
I AIN'T SCARED OF GHOSTS!
PUFF PUFF
...BUT THERE ARE WORSE THINGS THAT CRAWL OUT OF THE DARKNESS!
HUMAN BEINGS ARE ONE THING...
BWA HA HA!
AH HA HA HA
IT'S NOT FUNNY!
AND I WASN'T AFRAID AT ALL!
?!
JUST THE OTHER DAY, I MET A BLUE FIREBALL!
NO PROBLEM!
HEE HEE!
YURI, MONSTERS ARE WORSE THAN PEOPLE!
BECAUSE THEY REVEAL THE HUMAN HEART!
THAT WAS A RINKA.
BLUE FIREBALL?
HMM...

LATER, SHE BECOMES *YURI EGIN.*
SHE IS YOUR AND YUKIO'S MOTHER.
I...I KNEW IT!
TMP
AND NOW...
I DON'T GET IT, BUT I WON'T CAUSE ANY TROUBLE, OKAY?
??
That's just a sci-fi theory.
TIME PARADOXES WON'T OCCUR, BUT IT CAUSES CONFUSION.
YOU MUSTN'T INTERACT WITH PEOPLE IN THE PAST.
YA HA HA!
ACTUALLY, I KINDA LIKE IT!
THEY MIGHT GOUGE OUT YOUR EYES LIKE THEY DID TO OBABA!
THERE'RE DANGEROUS PEOPLE ABOUT.
THAT'S RIGHT.
YOU SHOULDN'T WALK AROUND AFTER DARK, YURI.
I'M COOL LIKE A PIRATE!
HEH
HEH
HEH
CHEEP

OKAAAY!!
YURI?
!
COME EAT!
YOU SHOULDN'T BE WANDERING AROUND THIS LATE!
NO WAY...
STAAARE
FWP
AGH!
?

WHERE ARE WE?
THE TIME AND PLACE AREN'T ALL THAT DIFFERENT.
DRIP
THIS IS A LOW-RENT DISTRICT...
...OF NORTHERN TRUE CROSS ACADEMY TOWN.
NORTHERN TRUE CROSS?
IT LOOKS KIND OF ROUGH.
FORTY YEARS AGO, IT WAS A DANGEROUS SLUM. HOMELESS PEOPLE AND CRIMINALS LIVED THERE.
!
IS THAT FATHER FUJIMOTO?
YURI!
KLNK
TP
TP
TP
TP

WHILE I'VE GOT TIME, I'LL BE YOUR GUIDE.
TROT TROT TROT TROT
...NO MATTER WHICH ERA YOU VISIT!
POOF
BESIDES, I'M THE KING OF TIME!
MY BODY MAY CHANGE, BUT MY IDENTITY DOESN'T...
BUT DON'T FORGET...
...THIS JOURNEY LEADS TO TRAGEDY.
ALL RIGHT...
KREAK
KLIK

LATER, YOU WILL KNOW HIM AS THE PRIEST, SHIRO FUJIMOTO.
WHAT THE...?
???
MEPHISTO?!
YOU CAME WITH ME?!
NOPE.
I'M JUST ME 40 YEARS BEFORE YOUR TIME.
FORTY YEARS?!
NO WAY! YOU DON'T LOOK ANY YOUNGER!
But your hair and clothes are weird.
DEMON VESSELS DETERIORATE, BUT THEY DON'T AGE.
Don't be rude.

JOLT
GAH!
SOMEONE BEHIND ME?!
WHSH
?!

...
HUFF
IS THIS...
...THE PAST?

Chapter 100: SsC00:40

Blue Exorcist Chapter 99: Beyond the Snow, Part 8

G

SAY GOOD-BYE...
HWOO
EWOO
KLIK
SWIP
...TO THIS CALM BEFORE THE STORM.

KAW
KAW
KAW
THE WORLD IS HEADED FOR DESTRUCTION, SO WHY ARE YOU JUST LAZING AROUND?
I KEPT MY PROMISE.
HMPH.
SO SOON?!
OH MY!
YOU IMPRESS ME, DOCTOR NEUHAUS!
DON'T WORRY.
THE PIECES HAVE BEGUN TO FULFILL THEIR FUNCTIONS.
PSHT

HATE?
HMM...
WHAT A HUMAN EMOTION.
BWSH
I CAN'T BELIEVE IT!
I CAN'T BELIEVE YOU DIDN'T TELL ME!
I HATE YOU!!
KRII
HM?
WHO COULD IT BE NOW?
KRII
KRII
KRI
IT IS COMPLETE.

GRAB
SHALL I REFLORB!! ?!
DESPITE YOUR CUSTOMARY IMPATIENCE, YOU DID WELL.
SWOO
...
AMAIMON.
HUH?
BOBBLE
BOBBLE
BOBBLE
BOBBLE
OHHH, YOU MEAN SHIEMI MORIYAMA? HA HA HA!
AMAI-MON ...
WHO IS THAT GIRL?!
...NOW YOU'RE ASKING ME THAT?
I CAN'T BELIEVE YOU DIDN'T NOTICE SOONER.
THE WORLD IS SUCH THAT WE CAN NO LONGER AVOID A FIGHT.
YOU HAVE LITTLE FREE TIME LEFT.

GRIND
"...ISN'T IN THE PAST."
"THE PAST IS WHAT YOU MUST ACCEPT."
GW
TMP
WELL THEN...
...MOVING ON!

I TOO AM WEAK.
...!
BUT YOU SAID...
...THAT YOU WANT TO BE STRONG.
IN WHICH CASE, YOU NEED TO UNDERSTAND YOUR CONDITION.
"UNFORTUNATELY, THE REALITY THAT YOUR BROTHER MUST ACCEPT..."

I KNOW ABOUT THE ILLUMINATI'S INHUMANE METHODS!
I WOULD NEVER SUBJECT MYSELF TO THAT!

I UNDERSTAND YOUR FEAR.

TAKE IT EASY...
...!!
AFTER ALL, I UNDERSTAND HOW YOU FEEL.

THE WEAK REJECT EVERYTHING AROUND THEM TO PROTECT THEMSELVES.
WEAK ?!
AND THAT IS ONLY NATURAL.

KING OF WATER? THIS THING'S ONE OF THE BAAL?!
PEEK
UH...
... I'M EGYN, THE KING OF WATER!
I...
I'VE HEARD ABOUT YOU FROM LUCIFER.
I'M THE ASSISTANT DIRECTOR OF THIS AIRBORNE LAB!
NO WAY!
EXAMINE ME?
FIRST, WE HAVE TO EXAMINE YOU...
... TO DETERMINE HOW YOU AND FATHER ARE CONNECTED.

GOOD MORNING, YUKIO.
DID YOU REST WELL?
LET ME INTRODUCE YOU TO MY YOUNGER BROTHER.
!
OH...
...G-GOOD MORNING!

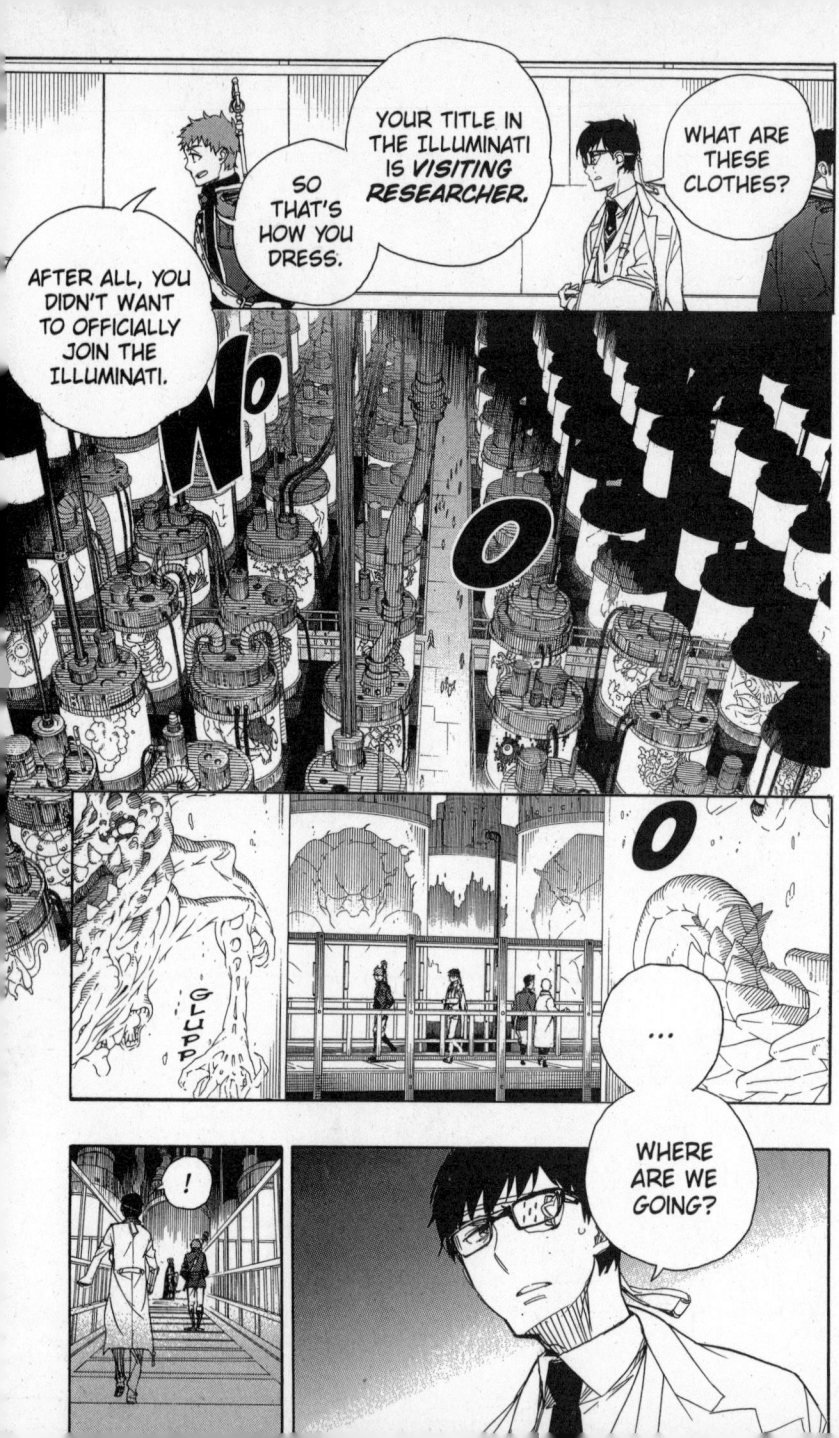
WHAT ARE THESE CLOTHES?
YOUR TITLE IN THE ILLUMINATI IS VISITING RESEARCHER.
SO THAT'S HOW YOU DRESS.
AFTER ALL, YOU DIDN'T WANT TO OFFICIALLY JOIN THE ILLUMINATI.
GLUPP
...
WHERE ARE WE GOING?
!

M
M
M
M
R

GURRRGLE

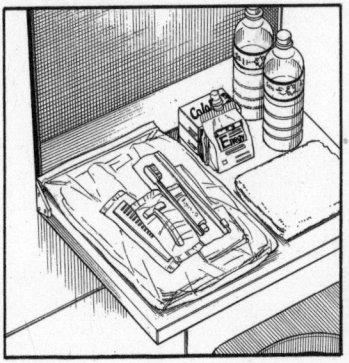

...
GRIN GRIN
JUST COME WITH ME.

I'M NOT A TEACHER ANYMORE.
NO WORRIES!

PSHH
...
...G'MORNING, TEACH!
OH...

OF COURSE!
...ARE THE WORST!!
YOU...
IT'S MY NATURE! I GOTTA GIVE IT TO THE ONE WHO DOESN'T WANT IT INSTEAD OF THE ONE WHO DOES!
NOW QUIT GRIPING AND GET GOING!
GN
O
O
SEE YA!
AFTER ALL, I'M A DEMON!

IT'S HILARIOUS! THEY SEE IT WITH THEIR OWN EYES BUT WANDER IN CONFUSION.
HUMAN BEINGS HAVE A WAY OF AVERTING THEIR EYES FROM REALITY AND TWISTING IT.
IF YOU WANT TO MOVE FORWARD...
...YOU MUST ACCEPT REALITY FOR WHAT IT IS.
...
THE PAST IS WHAT *YOU* MUST ACCEPT.
UNFORTUNATELY, THE REALITY THAT YOUR BROTHER MUST ACCEPT...
...ISN'T IN THE PAST.

IT WILL TAKE YOU...
...TO THE PAST THAT YOU DESIRE TO SEE.
HMM? HEE HEE HEE...
WHAT'S WRONG?
HEH HEH HEH! YOU SCARED?
YES, I'M SCARED.
I DIDN'T WANT TO KNOW ABOUT MY BIRTH IF I COULD'VE AVOIDED IT.
IF YOU WERE JUST GONNA REVEAL IT LIKE THIS, YOU SHOULD'VE TOLD YUKIO INSTEAD OF ME.
HE WANTED TO KNOW.
I ALREADY TRIED THAT MANY TIMES.
HUH?
BUT NEVER MIND!

AND SINCE YOU STILL CAN'T HIDE YOUR "HEART"...
POOF
?!
...I'LL DO IT FOR YOU.
HERE'S A FAREWELL GIFT.
IT'S A SPECIAL PATROL UNIFORM.
!!
IT'S MY OWN SPECIAL DESIGN!
IT'LL ALLOW YOU TO GO PRETTY MUCH ANYWHERE, AND IF YOU RAISE THE HOOD, IT'LL HIDE YOU LIKE A CAMO PONCHO.
CLOSE THEM ONCE...
...THEN INSERT THE KEY AND OPEN THEM AGAIN.
YOU CAN USE ANY DOOR.
THE LARGE GLASS DOORS TO THIS BALCONY HAVE AN INTERNAL LOCK.

W
ZZSH
FWOO
NO WAY...
THAT'S A KAMIKAKUSHI KEY.
I HAD IT THE WHOLE TIME?!
THIS?!
ALL IN DUE TIME.
EINS...
... ZWEI ...
... DREI!
AND IT'S THE ONE AND ONLY MASTER KEY THAT WILL TAKE ITS BEARER TO THE DESIRED DIMENSION.

HUH ??!
THE PAST AS IN THE PAST ?!
HOW?
YOU ALREADY HAVE THE MEANS.
THE KEY TO THE DOOR THAT WILL TAKE YOU INTO THE PAST.

KEY?!
I'VE GOT ONES FOR THE CRAM SCHOOL AND DORM, PLUS ONE FROM FATHER FUJI–
!

ANYWAY, I HAVE TO ADDRESS THIS SITUATION.
SO YOU MUST GO ALONE.
GO?
...
WHERE?
TO THE PAST.

RMM
RMM
RMM
BEHOLD!
RMM
RMM
RMM
THE ARTIFICIAL GEHENNA GATE HAS OPENED, THROWING THE WORLD INTO DISORDER!
AYIEEEH
WAAAH
AND IT'S ALL BECAUSE MY TACTICS FAILED!
BUT YOU CAN IGNORE THAT!
??
TACTICS ?!

I'M RYUJI SUGURO.
...ARE LIGHTNING'S APPRENTICE.
YOU...
BOW
SORRY TO BOTHER YOU WHEN YOU'RE BUSY...
YES, SIR!!
WE MOVE OUT AGAIN IN 30 MINUTES!
REORGANIZE THE TEAM WITH TAMERS PROFICIENT WITH THE AIR ELEMENT.
PALADIN!
...BUT I HAVE PROOF THAT LIGHTNING IS RIGHT!
GW

SHIEMI...
UM, WHO ARE YOU?
Sorry.
OH...
...RIGHT.
My apologies.
...YOU HAVE GROWN UP BEAUTIFULLY!
I BARELY RECOGNIZE YOU.
YOU HAVE YET TO REGAIN YOUR MEMORIES.
HEH HEH HEH...
...
BUT THERE IS NO RUSH.
YOUR MOTHER AWAITS.
THIRTY MINUTES !!!
SLAM

NO... WAIT!
WAIT!!!
BAM

W...
W- WHAT?
WHAT'S GOING ON?!
IT HAS BEEN A WHILE.

KAMIKI...
...THANK YOU FOR ALWAYS BEING SO NICE!
AND TELL EVERYONE ELSE THANKS TOO, OKAY?
W...
WHAT ...?

KACHAK
?!
...AND WE'VE COME FOR SHIEMI MORIYAMA.
WE'RE FROM THE GRIGORI AGENCY AT VATICAN HEADQUARTERS...
EXCUSE ME.
HUH?
WHAT?!
GIVEN THE CHAOS GRIPPING THE WORLD...
SWP
...WE AND YOUR MOTHER ARE WORRIED ABOUT YOU.
PLEASE, COME TO THE VATICAN IMMEDIATELY.
OKAY...
?!
HEY! WHO ARE YOU GUYS?!
WHERE ARE YOU TAKING HER?!
...!

SO COME ON...
SNIFF SNIFF
WHO ARE YOU?!
TELL ME!!
AFTER ALL, WE'RE... F... F...
...F- FR...
...FRIEN-
NOK
NOK
?!
NOK NOK

WAA-AAAH!
HUH?! WHY'RE YOU CRYING NOW?!
HOW SLOW-WITTED ARE YOU?!
I ALWAYS KNEW YOU WERE AN IDIOT!
Crying makes you ugly!
YEAH...
...I'M SUCH A DUMMY!
RUB
RUB
SOB
SOB
I ALWAYS LAG BEHIND EVERYONE ELSE!
I DIDN'T REALIZE IT UNTIL NOW...
...BUT NOW IT'S TOO LATE!
RUB
RUB
WHAT DO YOU MEAN?
TOO LATE FOR WHAT?
!
OOPS...
I CAN'T TAKE THIS ANYMORE!

DANG WIT ME SHIEN
...WHAT YOU MEANT BY "LIKE"?
OH NO NO NO! I'M SOOO EMBARASSED, I CAN'T BARELY LOOK AT HIM!
I'M SO
KSHUNEN
I...
...LIKE ...
SOB

LIKE RIN?
I KNEW IT. IT'S WARM.
JUST OUGHT BOUT YOU..
...I'VE DECIDED!
RIN...
ARE YOU ALL RIGHT?
!
O, M, NKS!
HUH?
THAT REALLY KEPT ME GOING.
THERE'S NOTHING FUNNY ABOUT THIS!

...WHEN I THOUGHT HE WAS REALLY GONE...
...I WAS SO FRIGHTENED!

IT SEEMS LIKE...
...YOU REALLY LIKE RIN.

...
ME?

...
HE ALMOST KILLED US...
...BUT THEN HE CAME BACK TO HIMSELF.
YOU'RE ALL RIGHT?
GOOD...
BUT BEFORE HE PASSED OUT...
...HE WAS GLAD WE WERE ALL RIGHT.
YES.
IT WOULD BE SAD IF MR. OKUMURA AND RENZO SHIMA...
...AND EVEN RIN OKUMURA ABANDONED US.
YEAH, I GUESS.
SIGH
I'M GLAD RIN CAME BACK.
THAT TIME...
I WANNA RELEASE ALL MY FLAME!
WAS THAT ALL HE HAD?

THE ARTIFICIAL GEHENNA GATE OPENED, SO EVERYONE STARTED SEEING DEMONS.
NOW THE WORLD IS IN MASS CONFUSION.
OH...
...TO RIN OKUMURA.
AND I HAVE NO IDEA WHAT WILL HAPPEN...
WHEN HE EXPLODED...
...I THOUGHT HE WAS GOING TO DIE. EVEN NOW, I CAN'T STOP SHAKING.
HE WAS LIKE A DIFFERENT PERSON.

THANK YOU, KAMIKI.
?!
N...
YOU'RE SO KIND.
I WOKE UP A LITTLE EARLIER.
YES! THANKS TO YOU!
SO IS EVERYONE ALL RIGHT?
YOU SHOULD GET MORE SLEEP. OR DO YOU WANT SOMETHING TO EAT?
SO WHAT HAPPENED?
TEE HEE...
NUH-UH! ANYONE WOULD DO IT. IT'S NOTHING SPECIAL!
WHAT ABOUT RIN?
YES.
YUKI IS GONE...
...ISN'T HE?
I THINK SIR PHELES HAS HIM IN CUSTODY.

POOF

K-SHUK

THANKS, BELIAL.
YEAH...
SHOULD ANYTHING ELSE ARISE...
...PLEASE SEND WORD TO ME.

SHIEMI...
YES ...?
?!
YOU'RE AWAKE?!

SIGH

KA CHAK
I'LL MAKE SURE...
...THE BROKEN KOMA SWORD GETS DELIVERED TO OSSAMA.
I SHOULD BE THE ONE TO DO THIS. THANKS, KONEKOMARU.
NO PROBLEM! A KEY WILL TAKE ME STRAIGHT THERE.
BYE.
CHAK
KA
トンズ
...
KACHAK
I SHOULD GO HANDLE THE MASTER'S BUSINESS.
THEN I'LL COME BACK. TAKE CARE OF MORIYAMA, KAMIKI!

THE FIELD OFFICE IS IN A PANIC.
I NEED TO GO HELP.

CHATTER
CHATTER
KINZO, STOP TALKING!
WHAT'RE YOU YAPPIN' ABOUT?! I CAN'T UNDERSTAND!
ONE AT A TIME!!
CALM DOWN AND FORM A LINE!!

MAMUSHI...
MOM, TAKE CARE OF MAMUSHI.

YOU JUST REST HERE.

NO.
IF IT'S AN EMERGENCY, THEN I SHOULD GO–
PAT

KLICK

I'M GOING TO THE FIELD OFFICE TOO.
I RECEIVED WORD THAT KONEKOMARU IS COMING.
WHAT ?!

OH... TATSUMA?
KLICK
KLICK

...BUT THERE ARE REPORTS THAT THE UNDERGROUND HOLDING TOWER WAS ATTACKED AND YUKIO OKUMURA DISAPPEARED FROM HIS CELL!
THE DETAILS ARE STILL UNCLEAR...
WHAT NOW?!
HUH?! WHY'S HE DOING THAT AT A TIME LIKE THIS?!
THE VATICAN HAS DETAINED SENIOR EXORCIST FIRST CLASS LEWIN LIGHT ON SUSPICION OF ASSAULT!
CAPTAIN KIRIGAKURE!
SPURT
WHOM
GAAAH! I ABSOLUTELY HATE THIS DESK WORK!!
MEPHISTO NEEDS TO GET BACK ON THE JOB!!
STOMP
DAY 2
CHATTER
HOW LONG DO WE HAVE TO WAIT?!
HELP US!
CHATTER
CHATTER
COME ON, HURRY UP!!

YOU MAY ALSO REPORT IT TO THE KNIGHTS OF THE TRUE CROSS.
HUH? IS THIS FOR REAL?
CONTACT WITH THE ANTISOCIAL ORGANISMS IS EXTREMELY DANGEROUS.
IF YOU SEE ONE, KEEP A SAFE DISTANCE AND INFORM YOUR LOCAL POLICE.

RAIL LINES HAVE SUSPENDED SERVICE, AND OTHER MEANS OF TRANSPORTATION HAVE BEEN DISRUPTED AS WELL.
IF ANYTHING HAPPENS, THEY'LL HELP US.
THE TAKARA GROUP HAS A PIPELINE TO THE KNIGHTS.
I'M SCARED, MOM!
DON'T WORRY. WE'RE SAFE INSIDE.
GOING OUT AT NIGHT IS ESPECIALLY DANGEROUS...
...SO PLEASE REMAIN IN YOUR HOMES IF AT ALL POSSIBLE.

CHATTER
CAN'T THEY USE PERSONNEL FROM ANIMAL CONTROL OR THE KEEP?
AND THE AICHI AND ISHIKAWA FIELD OFFICES ARE REQUESTING REINFORCEMENTS!!
THE POLICE AND SELF-DEFENSE FORCES HAVE REQUESTED ANTI-DEMON WEAPONS.
CHATTER
DIRECTOR!
I'M GLAD THEY FINALLY DECLARED A STATE OF EMERGENCY, BUT IT'S LITTLE MORE THAN A WARNING!
CAPTAIN KIRIGAKURE!!
THEY NEED TO ANNOUNCE SPECIFIC METHODS FOR WARDING OFF THE DEMONS!

TODAY, AT 11:30 P.M....
RRRING
...A SITUATION AROSE THAT FALLS UNDER SECTION 13 OF ARTICLE 2 OF THE SPECIAL PROCEDURES ACT.
RRRING
ANTISOCIAL ORGANISMS PRESS CONFERENCE
DUE TO NUMEROUS REPORTS OF ANTISOCIAL ORGANISMS AROUND THE GLOBE...
...THE JAPANESE GOVERNMENT HAS ISSUED AN EMERGENCY DECLARATION.
EMERGENCY DECLARATION
Panasonice
THE ANTISOCIAL ORGANISMS ARE EXPECTED TO CONTINUE SPREADING DISORDER.
緊急
宣言発令
速報
IN ACCORDANCE WITH THAT PROVISION, WE HAVE DECLARED A STATE OF EMERGENCY.
WE ADVISE THE PUBLIC TO REMAIN CALM AND REFRAIN FROM GOING OUTSIDE UNLESS ABSOLUTELY NECESSARY.
LIVE PRIME MIN
Prime Minister of Japan

THO
OM
GYAAAW
GYAAAW
THAT WON'T BE NECESSARY!!
SHALL WE PROVIDE BACKUP?
KZZT
KZZT
KZZT
AS IF AGITATED BY PEOPLE SEEING THEM...
...THE DEMONS ARE MORE VIOLENT AND DIFFICULT TO DEFEAT THAN EVER!
DAMN!
SOMEONE GET THE BYSTANDERS TO SAFETY!!
UNDER-STOOD.
BE CAREFUL.
GYAAAAW
BREAKING NEWS!!
AS PALADIN...
...I CANNOT ALLOW THIS TO HAPPEN!!

R
KAW
KAW
KAW
KAW
R
M
M
M
A flock of harpies?!
AT LAST, "ALL WILL BE ONE..."
KYAAAH
Ohhhh!
"...AND ALL EYES WILL SEE," HUH?
THE KNIGHTS ARE COMPLETELY FAILING TO KEEP UP.
WE HAVE THE GARDEN UNDER CONTROL.
WHAT IS YOUR STATUS?

NAC
Thursday,
THE CONFUSION AROUND THE WORLD HAS INSTIGATED THE LARGEST DROP...
...OF THE DOW JONES INDUSTRIAL AVERAGE ON THE NEW YORK STOCK EXCHANGE EVER RECORDED.
WE MUST NOT GIVE IN TO THE DEMONS!
IN THE CAPITAL OF SANTIAGO, PEOPLE CLAIMING TO HAVE SEEN DEMONS ARE SEEKING REFUGE AT A CATHEDRAL.
THEY'RE PANICKING!!!
DEMONS ARE APPEARING IN BROAD DAYLIGHT...
...SO NOW IS THE TIME...
...WHEN OUR FAITH MUST BE STRONGEST!
Wash
S. PRESIDENT S
Smith : U.S. President
WE MUST CONFRONT THIS CRISIS WITHOUT LOSING OUR HUMANITY!!
WHAT'S THAT?
?!
IT'S CLOSE!
FWAP
FORTIFIED BY THE BLESSINGS OF GOD, DO NOT FALL INTO DESPAIR...
...WHATEVER TRIALS MAY...
AMERICA AND THE HOLY SEE HAVE FINALLY ISSUED STATEMENTS.

Tweet
Miku
Crazy… My BF got eaten!
/01/03 15:10
260K RT 3,101 Likes
Karasu-karasu · 2h
Replying to:
U ok, Miku?
Anyway, stay safe!
2 11 23
Momomomo · 1h
Replying to:
No, she ain't ok! Wwwwwwww
1 9 28
https://www.mytube.com/watch?
Search
WHOA…
WHOA, WHOA, WHOA!!
KILL 'EM! KILL 'EM!!
367 418 SHARE
Joshua Brown
RECOMMENDED TRENDS
18:30
57%
Demons
1,012,864 Tweets
Antisocial Organisms
63,411 Tweets
Are antisocial organisms and demons different?
Mysterious Beings Spotted Everywhere
Government Recognizes Existence of Antisocial Organisms
Knights of the True Cross
misokatsu@Low_Altitude
What's this hashtag? #HowToDefeatDemons
Juddy@ 50s
Like holy water or something? #HowToDefeatDemons
More Veggies@GachaNoLuck
Smack 'em with a Bible! #HowToDefeatDemons
2 103 250
Kyoko Hashimoto, Society of Light 1m
Purify your body. And pray from your heart. This is the only way to keep away the servants of darkness. #HowToDefeatDemons
5 13
Kawata@ 1m
None of that's very convincing! #HowToDefeatDemons
1
Mii-kun "Check my new song! @
This is no time for goofing around! #HowToDefeatDemons
9 514 827

LICK
WHAT THE...?! WHAT IS THAT?!
A MOUSE?!
LICK
LICK
LICK
ACTUALLY, I'M A LITTLE NERVOUS...
OH, THAT'S NICE.
LANDING GEAR UP...
LANDING GEAR UP.
TONIGHT, I'M HAVING DINNER WITH MY DAUGHTER AND HER FIANCÉ.
LICK
LICK
BLEAT!
W
H
OO
M
KRASH
KYAH!
WHOA...
SKREEEEECH
KRASH
WE INTERRUPT THIS PROGRAM TO BRING YOU BREAKING NEWS.
BREAKING NEWS
THERE HAS BEEN A MASSIVE PILEUP IN THE CITY-BOUND LANES OF HIGHWAY A10...
NEWS
LIVE
ICN
24

KTN
K
GAAAH!
?
DON'T TELL ME YOU BELIEVE THAT STUFF! HOW DUMB ARE YOU?!
ANYWAY, DEMONS ARE EASY TO BEAT!
THOSE KINDS OF MOVIES CRACK ME UP!
LOOK, MOM!!
YIPEE
YIPEE
YOU SURE ARE HAVING FUN! WHAT ARE YOU DOING?
WHAT ARE THESE THINGS?
BUGS?
FRANÇOISE!
IT'S TIME FOR YOUR VITTLES!
YOU'RE LATE!
TWITCH
TWITCH
KA
IT'S A TRAPEZE ARTIST!!
KRASH
TCH!
AND IT'S STALE!
F...
FRANÇOISE ?!

After the Collapse of the Artificial Gehenna Gate
Day 1

Chapter 99: Beyond the Snow, Part 8

The Story So Far

Unknown to Rin Okumura, both human and demon blood runs in his veins. In an argument with his foster father, Father Fujimoto, Rin learns that Satan is his true father. Satan suddenly appears and tries to drag Rin down to Gehenna because Rin has inherited his power. Father Fujimoto fights to defend Rin, but dies in the process. Rin decides to become an Exorcist so he can someday defeat Satan and begins studying at the Exorcism Cram School under the instruction of his twin brother Yukio, who is already an Exorcist.

Rin and the others succeed in defeating the Impure King, awakened by the former exorcist, Todo. Meanwhile, Yukio fights Todo, and as the battle rages, he senses the same flame in his own eyes as his brother. Afraid, he keeps it a secret.

Later, mysterious events begin occurring around the globe orchestrated by a secret society known as the Illuminati. Finally, the Japanese government publicly recognizes the existence of demons.

Wanting to learn more about the flame of Satan in his left eye, Yukio goes to confront Mephisto. However, after an attempt on Mephisto's life, the Order arrests Yukio as a suspect. Rin goes to break Yukio out of confinement, but Yukio tells him goodbye. Rin attacks in a rage, but the Koma Sword breaks when he strikes, causing Rin's flame to blaze out of control. Shiemi manages to bring Rin back to himself. Realizing he needs to learn the truth about his and his brother's birth, Rin confronts Mephisto and demands the truth...

OSCEOLA REDARM

Another Arch Knight, he is an inspector at the Mexico Branch. He arrests Lightning for assaulting K.R.C. Laboratory Director Drac Dragulescu.

DRAC DRAGULESCU

An Arch Knight at the Romania Branch, director of K.R.C. Laboratory and former director of Section 13. Lightning has accused him of being connected to the Illuminati.

LUCIFER

Commander-in-chief of the Illuminati. Known as the King of Light, he is the highest power in Gehenna. He plans to resurrect Satan and merge Assiah and Gehenna into one.

SHIRO FUJIMOTO

The man who raised Rin and Yukio. He held the rank of Paladin, but Satan possessed him and he gave his life defending Rin. There is a possibility that he was a clone of Azazel created by Section 13.

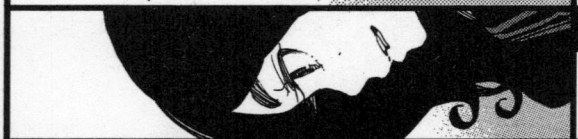

YURI EGIN

Rin and Yukio's mother. She conceived with Satan and died soon after giving birth. The Knights of the True Cross keep all information about her classified.

KURO

A Cat Sídhe who was once Shiro's familiar. After Shiro's death, he began turning back into a demon. Rin saved him, and now the two are practically inseparable. His favorite drink is the catnip wine Shiro used to make.

Konekomaru Miwa

He was once a pupil of Suguro's father and is now Suguro's friend. He's an Exwire who hopes to become an Exorcist someday. He is small in size and has a quiet and composed personality.

Izumo Kamiki

An Exwire with the blood of shrine maidens. She has the ability to become a Tamer and can summon two white foxes. The Illuminati had taken her captive, but with help from Rin and the others, she escaped and settled her grudge against the insane professor Gedoin.

Noriko Paku

An old friend of Kamiki. The two girls joined the Exorcism Cram School together, but Paku dropped out when she couldn't keep up. Now she takes classes in the general curriculum at True Cross Academy Private High School.

Shura Kirigakure

A Senior Exorcist First Class who holds the titles of Knight, Tamer, Doctor and Aria. Rin and Yukio helped free her from a contract entered by her ancestor.

Mephisto Pheles

President of True Cross Academy and head of the Exorcism Cram School. He was Father Fujimoto's friend, and now he is Rin and Yukio's guardian. The number two power in Gehenna and known as Samael, King of Time.

Lewin Light

An Arch Knight, he is Arthur's right-hand man as well as number two in the Order. An expert in Arias and summoning, he goes by the nickname "Lightning." He is performing an independent investigation into the Illuminati.

Cast of Characters

Rin Okumura

Born of a human mother and Satan, the God of Demons, Rin Okumura has powers he can barely control. After Satan kills Father Fujimoto, Rin's foster father, Rin decides to become an Exorcist so he can someday defeat Satan. Now a first-year student at True Cross Academy and an Exwire at the Exorcism Cram School, he hopes to someday become a Knight. When Yukio broke his Koma Sword, the power of Satan swallowed him, but Shiemi called him back to himself.

Yukio Okumura

Rin's brother. Hoping to become a doctor, he's a genius who is the youngest student ever to become an instructor at the Exorcism Cram School. However, the flame of Satan lies in his left eye. He has begun to question the righteousness of the Knights of the True Cross and has gone to meet the Illuminati.

Shiemi Moriyama

Daughter of the owner of Futsumaya, an Exorcist supply shop. She possesses the ability to become a Tamer and can summon a baby Greenman named Nee. She decided to quit the Exorcism Cram School, but she hasn't revealed the reason why.

Ryuji Suguro

Heir to the venerable Buddhist sect known as Myodha in Kyoto. He wants to achieve the titles of Dragoon and Aria. He is Lightning's apprentice and they are conducting an investigation together.

Renzo Shima

Once a pupil of Suguro's father and now Suguro's friend. Currently, he is a double agent providing information to both the Illuminati and the Knights of the True Cross.